Roade

THROUGH THE
CAMERA

Written and Compiled by Roade Local History Society

Front Cover: Syd and Derek Humphrey "helping out" in 1934

This page: Hartwell Road, looking towards Pear Tree House in the background, early 1900s

First published in 2009 by 'Roade Local History Society'

ISBN No: 978-0-9563496-0-6

© Roade Local History Society, unless otherwise indicated

Roade Local History Society, 5 Fox Covert Drive, Roade, NN7 2LL

Other publications: Roade Roll of Honour

www.roadehistorysociety.org.uk

In memory of Jean Hudson (1938 - 2004)
who was the inspiration for this book

Printed and bound by Elpeeko, Outer Circle Road, Lincoln LN2 4JY England
www.elpeeko.com

Supported by
 **The National Lottery**®
through the Heritage Lottery Fund

 heritage
lottery fund

Contents

Foreword

Bernard Donoughue

Roade is an ancient village with a history of which its inhabitants can be proud. With origins in prehistoric times, it is believed to have been settled in the Roman age and it is mentioned in the famous Domesday Book of 1086. For centuries it was primarily an agricultural village, but its working life changed when the railway came in 1838, bringing new employment and housing. Then in the twentieth century the Pianoforte Supplies factory (where my father worked for some 30 years) brought vibrant industrial life and relative prosperity. Now Roade has become mainly a dormitory for the county's modern service industries. So the village has, over the ages, been a mirror image of Britain's industrial and social development.

Roade does not immediately strike the visitor as having the picture-book beauty of the traditional English village. That is not its character. Its edges buzz with busy roads and roaring railway trains. An ageing factory and the extensive housing estates built since I was a child there can blight the view. But its inner core is pretty, with well -preserved houses nestling around the lovely church of St Mary. And its true heart is its people.

I grew up in Roade before, during and after the Second World War, a time which brought an influx of colourful London evacuees to enliven the village. It was over 60 years ago, but village life then is still vividly alive in my memory, as I am sure it is in the memories of surviving colleagues. All those earlier times are wonderfully recorded in this valuable photographic record

This book is a magnificent visual memorial to all aspects of Roade life. It is the real history of a true British community, conveying all aspects of village activity, from school to work, to sport, to prayer and to the pub. It will be of great value not only to social historians, but also to the elderly inhabitants of Roade who will enjoy the memories it stirs, to those in their prime who can be proud to live there, to the young who can here see what their forebears created, and to the as yet unborn who will be able to look back on all that went before them in their village.

We are grateful to Roade Local History Society and all who contributed to giving us so much pleasure with this fine book.

Bernard Donoughue

CHAPTER 1

Introduction

'It has long been a matter of regret to me that we hear so little of our local history…'

Thus the Revd. Maze Gregory, parish priest of Roade, opened his address to the Architectural Society of Northampton in February 1862.

He went on to give a succinct description of Roade parish and its history. He highlighted the unexpected fact that, even then, Roade had a highly mobile population, perhaps due to the advent of the railway station. *'From January 1 1854 to December 31 1861, eight years, there were no less than 200 changes, some houses having changed hands five times, and only 44 retaining their original inhabitants.'*

Nearly 150 years on, Roade shows much greater change. The number of dwellings has grown from 178 to around 990, the population from 664 in 1861 to circa 2,300 in 2008. Agricultural labour ceased to be the main occupation in the later 19th century and was vastly surpassed in the 20th century by Pianoforte Supplies Ltd. of Roade, which at its peak in the 1960s employed 1,800 people. The trend is now to less local employment with residents active in a broad range of businesses, particularly service industries, outside the parish. Though the roads have been improved this has led to much denser traffic, mainly on the already congested A508.

In the Revd. Gregory's day photography was a young art and early shots of Roade are rare. Today we have a plethora of means for recording all aspects of the village and its residents. Thanks to Bill Hudson a substantial database of photographs has been compiled and is still growing.

The saying 'one picture is worth a thousand words' is a cliché because it is true. This book is intended to give a visual flavour of Roade, to show some of its buildings, inhabitants and activities at different times, and some of the many changes undergone. It is hoped that further, more specialised books covering detailed aspects of life in Roade will follow.

Roade Local History Society is grateful for a generous grant from the Local Heritage Initiative, now administered by the Heritage Lottery Fund, which has made this publication possible.

The Revd. Maze W. Gregory, Vicar of Roade, 1853-66

"*It has long been a matter of regret to me that we hear so little of our local history...*"

CHAPTER 2

An Overview - Roade Through Time

Very little is known about early settlement in Roade. Archaeological evidence is sparse but some items from the prehistoric to Roman periods have been found in the parish. Roman coins and pottery were found in Roade before 1904 and in the 1920s and 30s a flint arrow head, an Iron Age ring and a Roman bronze pin were found in the Primary School garden. The evidence indicates that there were people living in the parish from prehistoric times but it is not clear how long the site of the village has been continuously occupied.

Letter to Miss Joan Wake (founder of the Northamptonshire Record Office) from Mr R W Janes, Headmaster of Roade Council School (now Roade Primary School), 1926

(NRO Roade Topographical Notes)

The placename 'Rode', from the Old English word 'rod' meaning 'a clearing in a forest', indicates a settlement in a wooded area in Saxon times. Domesday Book records a landholding for one plough occupied by two smallholders and some woodland at Roade and a larger area of 'waste' which later became the Hyde estate. Another landholding described in Domesday Book as in Courteenhall is likely to have been in the north-east of what is now Roade parish, around Summerale (or Summerhall) field. The oldest building in Roade, St Mary's Church, dates from the early 12th century, when it was owned by the Norman lords of Hartwell and Ashton. By 1166 the Hartwell family share had been given to the Augustinian Abbey of St James in Duston. The Abbey also owned land at Hyde, which it cleared and cultivated. The manor house (now Hyde Farm House) was built by the Abbey in the 14th century and had its own fishponds, water mill and open field system. Woodland around Roade was cleared and a 'township' grew up south of the church, surrounded by open fields. In 1301 21 households were assessed for tax or lay subsidy. In the 1520s about 30 people paid lay subsidy but there were probably more than 30 households as some would have been too poor to pay. Several estates held land in Roade (as did St James's Abbey) but it never had one overall landlord. It has always been an 'open village'.

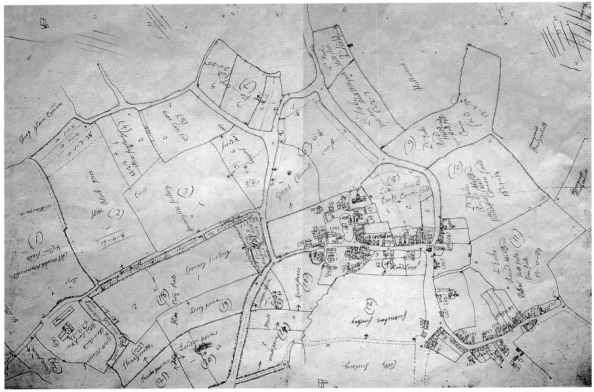

Grafton Estate Map, c.1720 *(NRO Map 447)*

The population increased in the 16th and 17th centuries and in 1674 79 households were assessed for hearth tax, of which 22 were discharged because of poverty. During the 18th and 19th centuries the most important landlords were the Dukes of Grafton, who owned around a third of the parish and around half the farmland. The earliest known maps of Roade were made for the second Duke of Grafton in the 1720s. Many of the old stone houses in the village are shown on these maps. Between the 1670s and beginning of the 19th century the population remained fairly static. The 1801 census recorded 345 inhabitants living in 82 houses in the parish. The late 18th century militia lists show that there were a number of craftsmen and tradesmen in the village as well as farmers and labourers. Some women and children supplemented their families' income by lacemaking.

MILITIA LISTS

At the time when the list opposite was produced, each county had to contribute a quota of men for service in defence of the realm. Parish constables (such as Robert Paggett of Roade) had to produce lists of eligible men. With the exception of peers of the realm, clergymen and ministers, articled clerks, apprentices, parish constables, seamen, and poor men with one or more children born in wedlock, all able-bodied men residing in the parish aged between 18 and 45 qualified for inclusion and were listed in their order of rank in the community. Men judged unfit to serve had their details of incapacity noted beside their name and profession. From the remaining pool the names of those enlisted, to serve for three years, were drawn by ballot. The initials against those drawn or exempted are those of Charles Newman and Thomas Beech, presumably Deputy Lieutenants for the county. Each enlisted man had a right to provide a substitute if he could, and this practice was very common. Peacetime service meant exercise and training under the colours for 28 days a year, usually in May and June, when the men were billeted in public houses and paid under a statutory scale.

Roade Militia List – 26 November 1796 *(NRO X270 1ZC)*

Northamptonshire to Wit …. for the Parish of Roade in the said County A Copy of Men from the age of Eighteen to forty five years by Order from His Majesty Deputy Lieutenants for the said County Novr. 26th 1796

	Thos. Marriott, Farmer		Wm. Sanders, Labour
X	Richd. Dent, Baker – drawn T.B. C.N.	X	Edmd. Evans, Labour – drawn T.B. C.N.
	<Jno. Kightley, Labour		Saml. Black, Shoemaker
	undersize – C.N. T.B.>		Thos. Walton, Labour
	Wm. Linel, Labour		Robt. Cave, Farmer
	Charles Carter, Sarvant		Jno. Ruff, Sarvant
	Wm. Black, Shoemaker		Thos. Hedge, Sarvant
	<Wm. Wilcox, Sheppard		Jno. Hedge, Baker
	Undersize – C.N. T.B.>		Thos. Mekens, Labour
	Wm. Geary, Farmer		Thos. Marriott Senior, Farmer
	Stephn. Warwick, Farmer		Nathn. Shewsbery, Taylor
	Thos. Cook, Mason		Thos. Warwick, Taylor
	Jno. Timson, Single man		Jno. Clark, Lacemaker
	Ed. Campion, Farmer		Wm. Hinds, Sarvant
	Stephn. Treen, Sarvant	C.N.	<Jno. Pinkard, Butcher
X	Thos. Westley, Colt breaker - drawn T.B. C.N.	T.B.	Blind right eye.>
	Wm. Rushel, Carpenter	C.N.	<Corus.[?] Gugen, Shoemaker
	Wm. Kightley, Single man	T.B.	Has[?] hare lip & ?.>
	Charls Hands, Shoemaker	C.N.	<Jno. Seaton, Labour
	Charles Hedge, Labour	T.B.	Lame in the foot.>
	Wm. Paggett, Farmer	C.N.	<Jno. Fearn, Labour
	Jos. Paggett, Farmer	T.B.	Hard[he?]aring >
	Thos. Bingham, Labour		
	James Clark, Labour		

Notice that all Persons who shall think themselves Aggrieved May Appeal Decr.1st 1796 at the New Whit Horse Towcester in the said County and that no Appeal will be Afterwards Received

1st Decr.1796 Verified on the Oath of
Robert Paggett Before us
        Chas. Newman, D. L.
        Thos. Beech, D. L.

        by Mr Robt. Paggett
        Constable

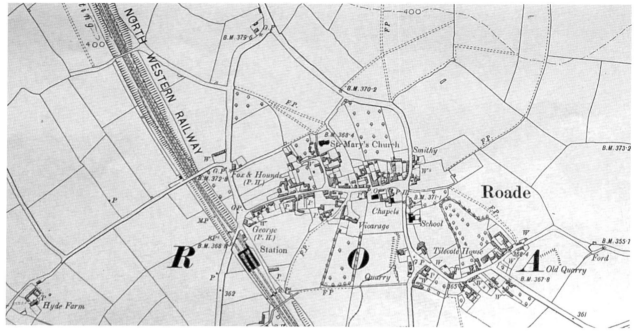

Reproduced from 1900 Ordnance Survey map with the kind permission of the Ordnance Survey

After the open fields were inclosed in 1819, the landscape around Roade was transformed but the village itself did not change much until the railway arrived in the 1830s bringing more jobs, houses and pubs. In 1861, just under half the men worked on the land and, by 1891, the proportion had dropped to around 18%. The population doubled between 1801 and 1841 and then remained around 660 to 700 until after World War II. The 1900 Ordnance Survey map shows Roade after the arrival of the railway and before the building of the factory at the end of The Leys. This opened around 1910 and became Pianoforte Supplies Ltd after it was taken over by Cyril Cripps in 1923. The Cripps family and their businesses were to have a major impact on Roade. The factory expanded until the workforce reached a peak of around 1,800 in the 1960s. The Cripps family became important benefactors and, although the factory in Roade has declined, their business has prospered elsewhere and is still a major landowner in the village.

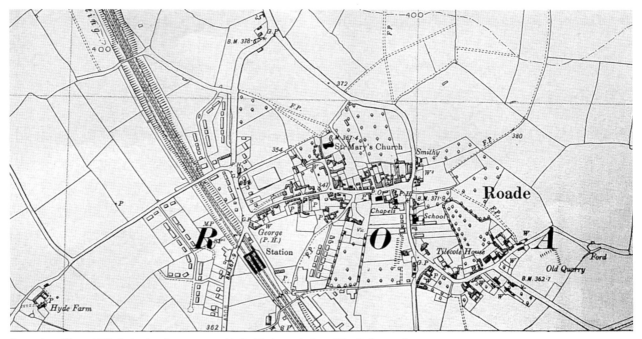

Reproduced from 1952 Ordnance Survey map with the kind permission of the Ordnance Survey

The 1952 Ordnance Survey map shows the factory and the first council houses in the village, which were built in The Leys in 1919. It also shows housing built to the west of the A508 during the 1930s and 40s. Expansion continued rapidly and the population grew from just under 1,000 in 1951 to just over 1,500 in 1961, peaking at just over 2,500 (850 households) in 1971. The railway station closed in 1964 but Roade remained an important service centre for the surrounding area, with a large secondary school, built in 1956.

Aerial photograph, 1995

After 1971, Roade's population declined slightly as families became smaller but the number of houses gradually increased to just under 1,000 by 2009.

Roade is still very much an 'open village' where numerous small businesses are based as well as larger ones. Although many people work elsewhere, recent surveys have shown that residents enjoy living in Roade and the village has a strong sense of identity and community spirit.

CHAPTER 3

Around Old Roade

We would now like to show you what residents and visitors would have seen at various times by taking you on a walk around old Roade.

The first thing a visitor arriving at Roade station (opened in 1838) would have seen was Station Road and The George Hotel.

The two rows of cottages, one directly behind The George and the other lower down Station Road, were both subsequently demolished.

Though the station was closed in 1964, trains on the busy West Coast Line and Northampton Loop still hurtle past through the cutting designed by Robert Stephenson (1838).

The factory, Pianoforte Supplies Ltd., benefited from the presence of the railway with use of its own siding.

Across the railway bridge carrying the A508 is Roade Main Garage which opened in the 1920s.

To the west, beyond the A508 and concealed by modern housing, is Hyde Farm House, the oldest vernacular building in Roade. This photograph is dated c.1900.

Farms also operated in the heart of the village until after World War II. The Elms farmhouse, halfway down the hill on High Street, is now a private house.

Houses and barns encroaching on High Street...

... were demolished in the 1960s and the road widened.

On the opposite side of High Street is Ivor Terrace and as you walk down the hill, further private houses.

At the bottom of the hill is Yew Tree Terrace, originally built to house railway workmen. The nearest house in the photograph, No 35, was the first Roade Methodists' meeting room in the 1840s.

The lowest part of High Street was prone to flooding before drainage improved.

A little further, opposite, near the corner of Church End, stood a village pump.

Warwick House, also on that corner, was the school house of the Misses Lea in the 1880s.

The Board reads "Warwick House School for Girls 4 Minutes from the Station".

Church End is a short cul-de-sac ending in a cluster of houses.

Construction of a new roof, changing the thatch to tiles. Croft Cottage was owned by Ron Tomkins who was later in partnership with Richard Shakeshaft, standing on the right of the group, c.1959.

St. Mary's Church, a Norman Foundation, stands on a slight rise approached by an avenue of pollarded limes.

A few yards further up High Street, past the post office, at the entrance to The Leys, a stand of mature horse chestnut and other trees cloaks the grounds of Roade Bowling Club. These trees lining the drive to the former Vicarage, which was demolished in the 1950s, are a magnificent sight with their masses of spring blossom.

Next are the former Baptist manse and chapel, both now private houses.

Opposite are three attractive thatched houses. In 1975, a fire in the thatch of No 28 - formerly Mrs Howard's cottage and Parish's shop, was thought to have been started by sparks from a bonfire.

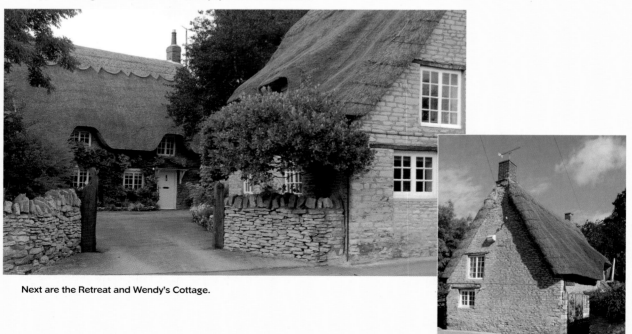

Next are the Retreat and Wendy's Cottage.

The White Hart is now The Roade House, a thriving restaurant and hotel.

At the top of High Street is a newsagent and store (once a private house, then a post office) and...

a terrace of shops, known as South View, now consisting of an office (formerly a butcher's), a haberdashery and a chemist with a hairdressing salon above. In the yard behind the remaining private house in the row, was one of the village bake houses, now empty.

Facing these is the Cock Inn, Roade's oldest and last-surviving pub.

High Street ends in a triangular green where it meets Northampton and Hartwell Roads.

Manor Farm, on the corner of Northampton Road, is now a private house.

Beyond the Cock, on Hartwell Road is the substantial, brick Methodist Church which celebrated its centenary in 2008.

Opposite the church is "The Old Manor House".

Manor Close is a 1960s estate built behind the house pictured (now demolished), with the water tower and cemetery behind.

A little further along Hartwell Road, the Primary School, built in 1876, has a complement of over 160 pupils.

Board Schools Roade.

The road forks at Memorial Green where Roade Feoffee and Chivall Charity owns four cottages (below right).

Opposite, just before the junction, is Stone House, built by local builder George Goodridge in 1880.

One road heads straight out of the village towards Ashton past an old nucleus of thatched houses,

Continuing along Ashton Road, we pass the former Barclays Bank sub-branch near the main gate to Pianoforte Supplies Ltd, scene of a failed raid, hence the police car in the photograph.

Ashton is reached by crossing the now-dismantled South Midlands Junction Railway the ('Scratter') on a hump-backed bridge.

Returning to Memorial Green, Hartwell Road bears south-east, taking a tortuous route past The Laurels Farmhouse on the right.

On the left is Pear Tree House which was the home of the Humphrey Family for several generations until 2008. The names of the proud owners of the cycles are unknown.

The Grove is a cul-de-sac off Hartwell Road just before
Tilecote House, a substantial villa built for Doctor W.H. Ryan in 1896.

Though the specimen trees are past their best, his 'Perspective' still stretches almost to the village cemetery, providing amenity to residents and benefit to wildlife.

Bretts Lane (formerly called Breech Lane and Bletch Lane), another cul-de-sac, diverges from Hartwell Road beyond Tilecote House. Passing Rose Cottage...

Breech Lane, Roade.

... and the original Burman's Farm house, locally known as Cozens' Farm,

the lane ends in a small, recently-built housing estate
on the site of the old farm buildings.

Continuing along Harwell Road, about a quarter of a mile further on, is Fox Covert Drive – a 1960s greenfield development beside the old SMJ railway bridge (subsequently demolished).

The saying 'one picture is worth a thousand words'

is a cliché because it is true.

CHAPTER 4

Churches

THE CHURCH OF
ST MARY THE VIRGIN

Photograph of St Mary's, c.1862 *(NRO NAS 53, p.104)*

A peculiar parish

The medieval parish of Roade included Ashton and Hartwell, with the mother church at Roade and chapels at Ashton and Hartwell. Roade church appears to have been established jointly by the Norman lords of Roade and Ashton and dates from the 12th century. It is not known whether there was an earlier church on the site. The Domesday survey of 1086 has no reference to a church or priest at Roade or Ashton but does record a priest at Hartwell. Roade, Hartwell and Ashton were closely connected and the Norman families who settled there usually had land in all three places. A mid 12th-century charter (witnessed by Stephen, priest of Roade) confirms that Simon de Hartwell gave St James's Abbey, Duston, the part of the church at Roade which belonged to his manor of Hartwell, together with some land, a mill and the chapel at Hartwell. Thereafter the Abbey owned two thirds of Roade church, while the remaining third belonged to the lord of Ashton, who provided a priest for (and received tithes from) Roade every third year.

This arrangement continued until the early 16th century when the lord of Ashton contrived to reverse the status of the Roade and Ashton churches, so that Ashton had a rector and Roade had a perpetual curate like Hartwell. After the dissolution of the Abbey, the two-third share of Roade church was acquired by the Fermors of Easton Neston, then by the Hoes of Hyde and others, ending with the Duke of Grafton in 1802. The rector of Ashton had to serve at Roade every third year or pay a curate to do so. In practice there was often more continuity than this arrangement implies, as the Revd. William Butlin served as curate (or vicar) of Roade from 1780 until his death in 1840. When the open fields were inclosed in 1819, the perpetual curate of Roade received an allotment of land in lieu of payment by the rector and the Duke. The rector was no longer responsible for providing a curate for Roade every third year and instead had the right to nominate every third vicar. The others were nominated by the Duke of Grafton until 1910, when the 7th Duke transferred his rights to the bishop of Peterborough. The benefices of Ashton and Hartwell were united in 1925, with the incumbent living at Hartwell. In 1987 Roade was reunited with Hartwell and Ashton, with the vicar living at Roade.

Early 20th century postcard

1 Statue of Madonna and Child

2 South doorway

3 Piscina

4 Medieval carved stone

5 Sanctus bell

6 Font

7 'Wake' tomb in the chancel

8 Holy water stoup

9 Bells taken from the tower for renovation

St Mary's through the centuries

The nave, chancel and lower part of the tower date from the 12th and 13th centuries although since then walls have been rebuilt, windows altered and replaced and roofs lowered and raised. Interesting early features are the Norman south doorway[2], the font[6], the 13th-century blind arcading on the outside of the tower, the piscina[3] (probably 13th-century but restored in 1857) and the holy water stoup[8] (transferred when the porch was rebuilt and now in a cupboard next to the outer door).

The top stage of the tower probably dates from the middle of the 15th century, when four bells were installed. These still exist although one was recast in 1727 and all were restored in 1950. An inventory of 1552 mentions the bells[9], including a sanctus bell which may be the cracked one[5] now kept in the chancel. During 19th and 20th century work on the tower, reused carved medieval stones[4] were found facing inwards. One of these is displayed in the chancel.

The plain tomb-chest[7] in the chancel is thought to be that of Richard Wake of Hartwell and his two wives, Dorothy Dive and Margaret Grey. Richard Wake died in 1558 and is known to have been buried at Roade with both his wives.

Before the Reformation, there were wall paintings and statues in the church and 16th-century wills include bequests for lights to Our Lady, St Katherine, the Rood and the Sepulchre and also for a banner cloth. During rebuilding in the 19th century, wall paintings were found but unfortunately not preserved. An ancient shelf on which a statue of St Mary would probably once have stood survived in the chancel next to the high altar. This now supports a statue of the Madonna and Child[1], after a design by Martin Travers, presented in 1954.

The earliest pictures of the church show the nave with a low, leaded roof and two square-headed windows, one of which had the date 1619 over it. The outline of the earlier high-pitched roof can be seen on the west wall of the tower. The earliest drawings and photographs also show the porch before it was rebuilt in 1864.

During the 19th century there was much rebuilding and alteration to accommodate the growing congregation. Between 1822 and 1864 the church was reseated and reroofed, the tower was repaired and the porch rebuilt. The north aisle was added in 1850, the vestry was built and an organ installed in 1879 and a Church Institute was built in the High Street (next to Warwick House) in 1885.

Mid 19th century drawing by George Clarke *(NRO NAS 50, p.118)*

An early photograph, c.1862

Mid 19th century watercolour omitting porch *(NRO NAS 53, p.104)*

Painting thought to be by the architect E F Law, showing the North Aisle built in 1850

Church Institute (built 1885 and demolished 1977)

The Victorian porch and vestry

The weathercock before installation in 1949.

Total weight of vane ¾ cwt, weight of bird 33lbs, total height 8ft 6ins. (In July 1982 the weathercock mysteriously disappeared but was found a few days later near Southam with three £1 notes and a message: 'My maiden flight was unsuccessful. Please take me home').

Church interior in 1929

New east window installed in 1958

Renovation in progress

In 1949 the tower was restored and crowned with a handsome new cockerel weathervane. The four ancient bells were renovated and rehung within a new steel bellframe with space for 6 bells. The interior of the church was refitted and redecorated in 1950. In 1952 a fifth bell was presented to the church by Mr (later Sir) Cyril Cripps to commemorate the restoration. Many gifts were made to the church around this time, including the stained glass east window with a legacy from Louisa Goodridge of Stone House in memory of her father, George Goodridge. It was designed by Christopher Webb and installed in 1958. A new church hall was built in 1972 and the old institute was demolished in 1977.

Interior in 1950 after restoration

The new high altar in the style of Sir Ninian Comper

The Blessed Sacrament Chapel after renovation

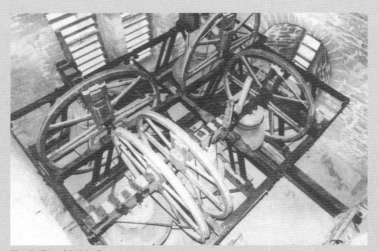

The Belfry with 5 bells

A sixth bell, dedicated to Lady Amy Cripps, was installed in 1979. A new west window, designed by Francis Skeat (a former pupil of Christopher Webb), was installed in 1986 in memory of Sir Cyril and Lady Cripps.

The 6th bell before installation in 1979

Vicars of Roade

Revd. W.H.Sharland
1908 - 1936

Canon N. Husbands
1941 - 1976

Revd. S.W.A.Gould
1976 - 1980

Canon C.H.Davidson
1980 - 1995

Revd. H. W. Webb
1996 - 2002

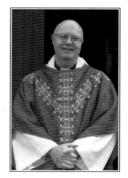

Revd. M. Burton
2002 -

Choir

Choir, circa 1910

Boys Choir in 1948

From left - Back Row: Alan Cozens, Tony Curtis, Bill Savage, Bernard Webster

Middle Row: John Collins, Peter King, Tony Baker, Clarence Puttnam

Front Row: Peter Tompkins, Charlie Wilson, Brian Bolton

Choir in 1978

From left: Susan Messenger, Joanne Phillips, Susan Hudson, Angela Lowe, Lisa Dredge, Stephanie Tipler, Jackie Hall, Paula Phillips, Tracy Doddington, Serena Nichamin

Bellringers

Bellringing Team, 1955

Left to Right: Alan Cozens,
Brian Wardale, Walter Richardson,
Tony Baker, John Sturgess

Bellringers, 1968

Left to Right: Tony Osborne,
Walter Richardson, Revd. Norman Husbands,
Josie Crow, Sandra Tompkins, Tony Baker

Bellringing Team, 1970

Left to Right: Eileen Stokes, Ray Moore, Chris Stokes,
Louise George, Anthony Stokes

ROADE BAPTIST CHURCH

Roade Baptist Chapel was built in 1737, although there had been a Baptist community in Roade since the late 17th century. A religious survey carried out in 1676 recorded 30 'separatists' in Roade. It is not known where the community worshipped before 1737 but baptisms took place in a stream at Hyde Farm and this practice continued until the beginning of the 20th century.

Although preachers could attract large numbers of 'hearers' from the surrounding district (about 200 in 1715), the number of fully committed members was much smaller and included people who believed in infant

Roade Baptist Chapel, c.1938

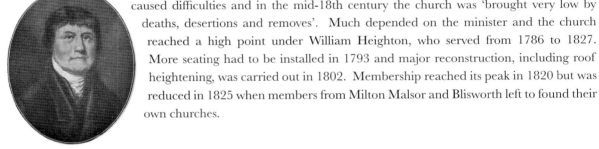

William Heighton

baptism as well as 'Baptism upon profession of faith'. Lack of funds and disagreements caused difficulties and in the mid-18th century the church was 'brought very low by deaths, desertions and removes'. Much depended on the minister and the church reached a high point under William Heighton, who served from 1786 to 1827. More seating had to be installed in 1793 and major reconstruction, including roof heightening, was carried out in 1802. Membership reached its peak in 1820 but was reduced in 1825 when members from Milton Malsor and Blisworth left to found their own churches.

Baptist ladies, c.1955

From left: Mary Robinson, Mrs Robinson, Mrs Tew, Mrs Nightingale, Eunice Jelley, Mrs Parish, Mrs Valentine, Mrs Every, Mrs Jelley, Mrs Horton.

Membership gradually built up again, although there were setbacks in the mid-19th century when the Anglican and Methodist chapels were both flourishing. In 1871 the chapel was reseated and a new schoolroom was built. The burial ground next to the church was extended two years later. By the end of the 19th century the church was in difficulties again and for part of the early 20th century Roade had to share a minister with the Milton and Blisworth churches. However, the church was supported by some dedicated members who helped to organise a variety of activities, such as fetes, the Band of Hope, Mens' Fireside, Ladies' Bright Hour and, of course, the Sunday School. Ray Parish remembers going to chapel three times every Sunday in the 1930s.

'Fireside' Outing to Derbyshire, 1950s
From left - Back row: Brian Sturgess, Donald Abbott, Tony Curtis
Front row: Clarence Puttnam, Charlie Wilson, Richard Johnson, Bernard Webster.

Sunday School lads on a trip to Wicksteed Park in the 1930s
From left: Ray Parish, Walter Coles, Bill Ashby, Ray Battams, not identified, Geoff Clarke, Stan Hawkins

Fete, 1963

Many people will remember Mr Ray Lineham, who became the part-time lay pastor in 1948, and also his wife Flora who ran the Band of Hope and other activities. In spite of their efforts, the congregation gradually dwindled. In the 1980s the building had to be closed as unsafe, although Mr Lineham continued to hold services in private houses. Mr Lineham died in 1993 and the church was sold in February 1994. For a while the former chapel was a guest house but it is now a private residence called the Chapter House.

Group in front of manse - Mr and Mrs Lineham seated centre

ROADE METHODIST CHURCH

Wesleyan Methodism in Roade owes its origins to a group of navvies from Bletchley who came to Roade to work on the railway cutting. At first they attended the Baptist chapel, but their enthusiastic "alleluias" during sermons proved unpopular and they began worshipping in a room at the end of Yew Tree Terrace, registered in October 1834. To avoid mockery from locals, who found their mode of worship somewhat alien, they moved to a house in Barn Close (location uncertain) registered in April 1835. As the congregation grew, a further move became necessary to a former malthouse between two cottages in Ashton Road. The chapel opened in April 1852 and could seat 80.

Methodist chapel (centre) in Ashton Road

Ashton Road chapel interior

As membership continued to expand, a new chapel, designed by S. J. Newman and seating 180, was opened in 1875 next to The Cock Inn.

In 1908 a new chapel of the same capacity, designed by Brown & Mayor, was built at right angles to the former one and linked to it by a porch. The old chapel was converted to a schoolroom.

Chapel opened 16th September 1875

1908 chapel (left) with earlier 1875 chapel (right)

Chapel interior, 1908

Methodist group at Yew Tree Cottage, 1894

Tea party

Sunday School

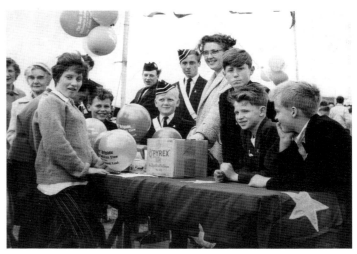

Boys' Brigade, 1961

Duke of Edinburgh award presentation, 1975

Fete, 1963

Choir, 1964

In the twentieth century the chapel was a focus for many activities, including Sunday School, Woodwork Centre, Boys' & Girls' Brigades and Youth Club, but only the first still continues. Despite this, and a decline in the number of worshippers, the chapel was still vigorous and the complex underwent extensive refurbishment in 1994. Today it is in active use by the congregation, and as a setting for concerts and other leisure activities.

Mrs Higgins on bicycle with her daughter, Mrs Ethel Humphrey, late 1940s

Prominent members of the congregation have included:

Mrs Elizabeth Higgins 1858-1954

Mrs Higgins is said to have 'dedicated her life to the cause of Methodism in Roade and surrounding villages'. She was christened in the old chapel in Ashton Road and remembered attending services there as a small girl. At that time very few people could read and so the hymns were read out and sung two lines at a time to the accompaniment of a flute.

Charles Kightley, c.1940

Charles Kightley 1889-1968

Charles Kightley served as Trustee, Trust Secretary, Sunday School Superintendent, Chapel Steward and Society Steward and was also Chairman of Roade Parish Council. His nephew, Bert Kightley, and his son and daughter-in-law, Bill and Madge Kightley, were also very active members of the church.

Syd Humphrey, c.1940

Sydney (Syd) Humphrey 1921-2007

Though Syd had many private interests – he was an expert lepidopterist, philatelist and fancy-bird breeder, sang in Oratorio and researched genealogy – his Christian faith dominated them all. He was accredited as a local preacher in 1950 and only retired in 1990, was Church Council Secretary for thirty years and, with his brother Derek, taught in the Sunday school for over sixty years. He is sadly missed by his friends in the congregation and village.

ST LAWRENCE'S CATHOLIC CHAPEL

The Catholic chapel of St Lawrence in Croft Lane, 1982

A centre for Mass at Roade had been established in 1954, served by priests from the Cathedral in Northampton, and Mass was said for a while in "The George" public house. On 7th October 1962, the chapel of St Lawrence was opened in Croft Lane, serving a wide area of South Northamptonshire. As there was no resident priest at Roade, Cathedral clergy continued to officiate at the chapel until the 1970s, when a priest from Newport Pagnell, 14 miles away, took over. In September 1981 a priest was based in Far Cotton to serve the expanding Southern District of Northampton and he took on responsibility for Roade – only 6 miles away. By this time there was a regular congregation of about seventy worshippers – some coming from Wootton and Blisworth as well as from Roade.

On 19th November 1989 a new Catholic church opened in East Hunsbury, which was better able to serve the whole area and within a few months St Lawrence's was closed. The internal furnishings were removed and transferred to the new church. The Diocese arranged for the redundant building to be let to a firm of solicitors for storage and external signs of its former ecclesiastical use, the Cross and Notice Board, were progressively removed. Outline planning consent has since been given for conversion to a dwelling.

'Three of his children are at the lace school, and, besides paying

for the thread and schooling, earn about 6d. per week'

Sir Frederic Eden writing about the family of Richard Walker of Roade in
'The State of the Poor', published in 1797.

CHAPTER 5

Schools

EARLY SCHOOLS

Before the Board School (now the Primary School) opened in 1876, education in Roade was voluntary. Fortunate boys attended the Grammar School at Courteenhall, while some children went to various local church or private schools. Others received some basic education at lace schools and Sunday Schools.

Church School (now 7 Church End)

7 Church End

By the mid 19th century a Church of England school had been established at 7 Church End. Evening classes, entertainments and parish meetings were also held at the school. According to the Roade Church Almanack, in 1866 the Night School *'was not opened until Nov. 22, owing to the prevalence of small pox in the village, and then only for boys attending the Sunday School. For the same reason, all evening entertainments have been suspended. N.B. - Read the paragraph on Vaccination.'* In the mid 20th century the following text was found on one of the walls of 7 Church End: 'REMEMBER THY CREATOR IN THE DAYS OF THY YOUTH'. The school closed in 1876 when the new Board School (now the Primary School) opened in Hartwell Road.

Baptist Church School
(now part of the 'Chapter House', High Street)

Baptist Church - school room at end right

Herbert House Seminary
(now 6 High Street)

Former Herbert House Seminary

In the early 19th century a school room and vestry wing was built at the west end of the Baptist Chapel. In 1841 it was recorded that one day school and one Sunday School were being run by the Baptists in Roade and that the number of students had increased since 1835. There was also a vestry lending library at that time. The day school ceased during the 19th century but Sunday school classes continued until the mid 20th century .

The Herbert House Seminary for Young Ladies was opposite the Baptist Chapel. It was founded at some time before 1849 by Miss Anne Louisa Lalor, who was joined by Miss Mary Wilson (previously a teacher at the church school). There were some boarders, as well as daygirls, and lacemaking was taught in the evenings. The school closed in 1879. The two teachers were buried in the same grave in the Baptist graveyard - Miss Lalor in 1886 and Miss Wilson in 1906.

Warwick House School group, c.1900

Warwick House (2 Church End)

Warwick House is named after Stephen Warwick, a prominent Baptist who bought the house in 1793 and also owned Hyde Farm. A 'ladies' school' was established there about 1880 by the Lea sisters, Louisa and Emma. It was known as Warwick House School for Girls or Roade Boarding School and was still being run by Miss Emma in 1914. There were dormitories on the upper floor of 4 Church End and an adjoining door between the two houses (later blocked off). The stables and coach house were on the opposite side of the High Street and now belong to Uplyme Cottage. A sign outside stated that the school was '4 mins from the station'.

Warwick House in 2007

ABOUT
896
I SHOULD THINK

67. Burghley Road
LONDON N.W. IS THAT CORRECT

My dear little dinksies,
I have heard that you were at Roade, and that Mamma & Dada are at home. Fancy you being away from mamma, and out in the country all alone. I hope you are both good girls, and are Kind to Miss Lee, who is taking such care of you. Winnie must eat and get quite strong, and Bertha must take of her hand, and walk along like little ladies. How are the piggies in the sty? Do they grunt, and

ask for their dinners? How nice it was for dada to come over and see you on Sunday. What does little Mary do without you. She has to play all alone, and look after the dolls. I hope she keeps them quite clean, and feeds them well. The dinksies will hardly know you again, when you go home. Be good girls to each other, and then mamma will be glad. I send you a lot of kisses from Aunt Edith.
This is from your
Uncle Walter

Letter to the Teal sisters at Warwick House School, c.1896

Warwick House School,
ROADE.

Certificate of Excellence awarded

to Miss May Martin

for attaining the highest number of marks in the School Class,

for Writing, Arithmetic, and Drawing

during the term ending Easter 1900

Principal: Miss Lea.

Certificate awarded to May Martin in 1900

PRIMARY SCHOOL

The original buildings which are still in use today

Roade Board School
(later Roade Council School, now the Roade Primary School)

Roade Board School, as it was known, opened its doors to 77 children, between the ages of 5 and 13, in 1876. It was managed by a Board consisting of three 'Churchmen' and two 'Dissenters'.

Seventeen years later, the original building was extended to house the growing number of children attending the school. In 1985, Mr Tyrrell, the headmaster, wrote in the school log - *'It is interesting to record that written on*

the back of a piece of wood used as a batten for clothes pegs that had been removed from the old cloakroom space in the Victorian block were the words J. Webb. Hanslope 1893 Whitbread Builder Contractor. This school enlarged 1893 at the cost of £710.0s.0d'. The county council took over the school in 1903, when there were about 140 pupils.

The first head teacher, John Brown, was succeeded in 1879 by James Elden. It was he who established the school garden in 1907, introduced woodwork for boys in 1911 and cookery for girls in 1917. In 1925 the Methodist schoolroom across the road (where Sunday school classes were held) was leased and used to teach the older boys woodwork and the girls cookery.

At this period, Roade pupils were winning the County Gardening Shield virtually every year and competed successfully at music festivals and in essay competitions.

Under Mr Maxwell (1934 – 1951) the school continued to be highly successful in sporting competitions, Music and Gardening.

Mr Elden with school group, 1916

Roade School gardening team, 1926

An extract from a Board of Education Inspection Report on 22 June 1938 reads:

'....*The record of the school in Music is high and in Sport it has done well: the Headmaster himself has a reputation in both these subjects. The school garden is an outstanding feature, for besides being a beautiful place in itself, it provides a wide range of instructional possibilities; the utilitarian part is kept in proper proportion and improves rather than spoils the picture. Perhaps this school is unique in the county in providing Gardening for all classes from the Infants upwards.....*'

Mr Maxwell and the school sports team, 1935

Group photo with Bernard Donoughue sitting fourth from left in front row. Also in the group are Emily and Rita Shipman, John Coles, Bernard Webster, Jacqueline Douglas, Margaret Lane, Ralph Wallace and Rosemary Curtis, 1940.

During World War 2, evacuees more than doubled the school roll. Pupils were placed in every available room around the village. There were classes in the Church Institute, the Wesleyan Chapel, the Baptist Chapel Room and a nursery class in the George Inn. However, by 1945 most evacuees had returned home and numbers dwindled until the school was able to accommodate all the children again.

Numbers rose again as new houses were built, the school leaving age was raised to 15 and older children from surrounding villages attended the school for their final year until Roade Secondary Modern School opened in 1956. The problem was solved by erecting HORSA (Huttings Operation for the Raising of School-leaving Age) Huts on the playground.

Group of children evacuees outside the Church Institute

School group with Mr Harper, c.1950

In the 1950s and 60s sport again played a major role in school life and many shields were won. Pupils were also successful in gaining places at Towcester and Northampton Grammar Schools. Indeed, so many pupils went on to Grammar School that in1952 there were no Roade boys in the senior class.

School Group photo, 1958

Roade Primary School Group c.1956

Left to right -

Back row: David Chambers, Ray Moore, Paul Parrish, Norman Green, Jimmy Oakey, Paul Gibbs, Stephen Webster, Jeffrey Osborn, Peter Alliot, Reggie H (?)

2nd row from back: John Saul, Elizabeth Gledhill, Edda Mancini, Pauline Gray, Linda Frost, Gillian Roberts, Rita Hawkins, Margaret Ager, Heather (surname not known), Patsy Barber, Bobby Garwood

3rd row from back: Frances Cowley, Susan Morris, Josephine Whitlock, Teresa Wroughton, Headmaster - Mr Hall, Jenny Goodridge, Linda Johnson, Brenda Walker, Susan Robinson.

Front row: Christopher Stokes, Leslie Wilson, Noel Sheldon, Frank Spraules, Keith Luck

Members of the 1966/67 season Football Team

Left to right - Back row: Richard Hillyard, Philip Davies, Ian Curtis, Christopher Herbert, Vyvian Buswell, Brian Battams, Ian Atkins, and Mr Curtis (teacher)

Middle row: Alan Perkins, Stephen Coles, Kevin Elliot, Compton Johnson, John McNamara, Walter Norman and John Inwood

Front row: Norman Robins, Leslie Robinson, Philip Howard, Richard Horton, Raymond Waskiw and Jimmy Bolton

The 1988 Cricket Team

Left to right – Back row: Mark Brough, Neil Collier, Christopher Sawbridge, Neil Howard, Graham Frost (teacher), Stephen Hurst, Simon Willis and James Curtis. Front row: Stephen Martin, Matthew Clayson, Ross Mawby, Neil Hayhurst and Andrew Threlfall

The School Netball Team, 1975/76

Left to right – Back row: Diane Frost (teacher), Rosemary Middleton and Susan Russell. Front row: Susan Hudson, Megan Fitchett, Tracy Carr, Jean Saunders, Janet O'Brien, Joy Packer and Karen Wickens

The Netball Team in 1981

Catherine Jones chaired by her team mates after scoring the winning point in an 8-7 win over Blisworth School. Members of the team include Tracey Dredge, Rachel Case, Julie Mann, Nichola Springer and Joanne Danvers.

In 1964 the LEA proposed to completely rebuild the school, in two phases, followed by demolition of the old buildings. However, the Victorian building was retained when the new building was completed in 1971.

In 1982 there was significant damage to the old Headmaster's schoolhouse (converted into the caretaker's house in 1957) when a fire occurred in one of the bedrooms. Part of the roof was damaged in the blaze and the office below the bedroom suffered water damage.

The building programme continued during Clive Geddes' headship (1990 – 2000). The Lineham block (named after Ray Lineham, a long serving Chair of Governors) built with a £350,000 Government grant, was completed in 1996 and the HORSA huts finally demolished. In 1999, new classrooms were constructed in the vacant caretaker's house. The largest of these has been rented out to the Bumble Bees Pre-school Group, since 2001.

Fire at the Primary School, 1982

In 2000 a dedicated team of staff, parents and pupils led by teacher Mrs Francklow and her husband, created a small garden to commemorate the millennium in the original school house garden. The garden was designed to be a quiet area for pupils.

The school celebrated its 125th Anniversary in June 2001 and five of its oldest, former pupils, Sydney Lenton, Edna Abbott, Hilda Lenton, Nora Bolton and Gladys Savage, were invited by head teacher Helen Hollwey to join the celebrations.

Today, under the leadership of Alison Bailes, Roade Primary remains forward looking. Despite falling rolls, due to new schools opening in nearby villages, the school provides an exciting curriculum whilst concentrating on a good grounding in basics. Standards continue to rise and the school is forging strong links with the wider community.

Mrs Kinnock officially opening the Lineham Block, 1996

A parent working in the Millennium Garden, 2000

125th Anniversary Celebrations, 2001

SECONDARY SCHOOL

Roade Secondary Modern School, 1956

Roade Secondary Modern School
(later Roade Comprehensive, now Roade School Sports College)

The L.E.A.'s policy of transferring older children from small, non-provided schools elsewhere in the district to Roade (the only former board school in the area) meant that Roade Primary School had a large senior class. Therefore, the village was an obvious choice as the location for a secondary modern school.

The school, built on a nine acre site on Stratford Road, opened in September 1956 with just over 330 pupils aged 11 to 14. The poppy was adopted for the school logo as they grew in such abundance in the field on which the school was built. Within two years the number of pupils had reached 426. The growth was partly the result of the post-war bulge, but also as a consequence of the decision to build large numbers of local authority houses in Roade and some of the other villages served by the school. In 1960 staffing rose to 20 teachers with the completion of a major extension.

The Headmaster, Graham Ford, retired in 1976 after 20 years service; he was followed by Ian Willison who himself led the school for almost twenty years.

In the early 1960s the school formed links with the Realschule, Katzenelnbogen, which is situated in the

Poppyfields once covered the site of the Secondary School

German School visit, 1978

Ian Willison and Will Adams with teaching and support staff c1993

Reinland Pfalz district of West Germany; groups of German students regularly visited Roade and vice versa. Student exchange visits were also arranged to Lusignan in the French Department of Vienne. However, these visits were discontinued a few years ago.

The school was re-designated a Comprehensive School in September 1975, when the age range was extended to 18 years. A Sixth form was gradually developed and, from 1982, had its own block of classrooms.

In the following decade the school acquired an excellent academic and social reputation; this, together with a Government decision to allow open enrolment, led to another increase in the school's population.

Will Adams joined the school in 1982 as a Deputy Head and was appointed Headmaster in 1993. During his period of headship he named different areas of new buildings and sports fields after former students, staff, governors and people who had formed close associations with the school. Some examples are: *Husbands Hall*, named after Canon Norman Husbands who was the Chair of Governors for many years; *Stubbs Study*, named after Dr. John Stubbs, a village correspondent and school governor; *Canvin Way*, after Ian Canvin, an architect; *Capel Field*, after

Sister Frances Dominica, the founder of Helen House, the children's Hospice in Oxford, receiving a cheque for £1,460 raised by pupils of Roade Comprehensive School, 1982

Will Adams, Headmaster, with pupils, 1996

Lord Donoughue officially opening the Willison Centre

Minister of Sport's visit to Sports College, 2001

David Capel, ex pupil and Northants County and England cricketer, and *The Donoughue Room* named after Lord Donoughue, who grew up in Roade and is patron of the Willison Centre.

When the Willison Centre, named after the school's second Headmaster, was completed in 1994, it made possible the far wider use of much better facilities for activities, both sporting and non sporting, outside school hours. Although the school had functioned from its start as an evening institute, the Centre provided even greater opportunities for the wider community.

1994 also saw the completion of a £2.75m building programme and a floodlit, multi-sports park. When Derek Redmond, ex pupil and Olympic runner, was invited to switch on the floodlights for the astroturf sports field, he, Sharon Davies MBE (whom he married in 1994) and John Regis MBE, his team mate at the 1991 World Championships in Tokyo and Olympic silver medallist, ran to the ceremony from Hunsbury (and presumably back again afterwards!).

In September 2000 the school achieved its Specialist status in sport to become the only Sports College in the county at that time. The purpose of specialist schools is to raise academic standards; in Roade's case the medium is sport.

Whilst on a flying visit to Northampton the following February, Kate Hoey, the then Minister of Sport, visited the school to see the new sports centre. The school was re-designated as a Specialist Sports College in 2004.

On 1st January 2005 the school was granted Foundation status. It also has recognised status as an initial teacher training centre and, in conjunction with

Derek Redmond presenting the winners' Certificates to the South Northants and District Championships Under 13 District Champions'. The Roade School winners proudly holding their Certificates are: Robert Harris, Piers Walker, Alex Canvin, Richard Wiles, Matthew Wright, Colin Dobson, Oliver Payne and Timothy Rowkins

other schools in South-West Northamptonshire, offers a Postgraduate Certificate of Education qualification through the University of Leicester.

On September 4th 2006, Roade Sports College celebrated its 50th anniversary with the planting of five golden rose bushes, one for each decade. Among those at the ceremony were David Goode, one of the first pupils on roll, Denise Russell, teacher, Ross Parkinson, head teacher from 2005, ex teachers Mike Sherry, Roger Martin and Orland Humphrey and the two youngest pupils at the school Gareth Elliott and Abi Moxham.

Roade School Sports College is justly proud of its achievements during the last 50 years. Many local families have a long association with the school and today a growing number of ex-pupils are forming links with the school as parents of pupils attending Roade School.

50th Anniversary Celebration, 2006

CHAPTER 6

Doctors

Little is known of the early Roade Doctors, such as John Ward and William Cummings, who were 'surgeons' in the village in 1849 and 1854 respectively. However, a little more is known about Richard Orpen. He came from Ireland with his wife and sister in 1875 and lived in *'a fine stone house'*, believed to be 'Hillcrest', in the High Street. Four of his children were born in Roade and he died aged 43 in 1888.

Dr Walter Henry Ryan was born 3rd May 1853 in County Limerick, Ireland, and came to Roade in 1888. He later built Tilecote House at the junction of Hartwell Road and Bretts Lane. The Surgery was an outbuilding in the garden and it is said that patients had to wait outside *'come rain or shine'*. One of his two sons, Captain James H A Ryan, was killed in the 1914 - 18 War. Dr Ryan was quite a character and a good all round sportsman. He kept horses and was a keen huntsman. He had his own cricket team and a *'gentleman's cricket pitch'* near the old quarry on Stratford Road. He was Medical Officer for Hardingstone Workhouse. Dr Ryan died in 1927, his wife in 1933. Soon after Dr Ryan died, the goodwill of the practice and the old "Fox and Hounds" was bought by a Dr Jeaffreson of Blisworth. He employed an assistant, a Dr Sullivan, and then a lady, Dr Wharton. In 1931 he took a Dr Maguire into partnership who started a twice weekly surgery at Ashton.

Dr W H Ryan

By 1936, however, they both felt that the practice was not really big enough to support two doctors, so the partnership was dissolved. Dr Jeaffreson then employed a Dr Theron until Dr W.A. Clements bought the practice in 1939.

Dr Clements was a qualified dentist but had to abandon dentistry after nearly 20 years, due to injury sustained in a motoring accident. He then made a courageous decision to re-train and qualify as a doctor. He practiced alone during the war years, serving both Blisworth and Roade.

Dr Maguire

Above: Dr W.A. Clements in 1955

In 1946 Dr Clements was joined by his newly qualified son Stephen. Within a week, Dr Clements senior had to enter hospital in London and Dr Stephen was left to manage the practice by himself. Dr Stephen and his wife later moved to the house adjoining the Surgery. Mrs Clements took messages and phone calls and dispensed medications prescribed by her husband. In his absence she was often asked for advice on urgent problems. There was little free time and they were

Left: Dr Stephen Clements addressing Roade Local History Society in 2007

almost continually on duty. There were limited night calls in the beginning as few people had access to a telephone or car, so messengers had to walk or cycle to the doctor's house. Dr Clements held surgeries once or twice a week in other villages where residents would allow him to use their houses for consultations.

A tragic event occurred in 1969 when two trains collided in Roade Cutting. The driver of a passenger train was trapped behind his controls, seriously injured. The only access to the track was by descending a long ladder attached to the wall of the cutting which Dr Stephen said was perilously close to the overhead electric power lines. He squeezed through the overturned first coach to reach the driver but could not save him. He died shortly afterwards.

The 1969 train crash, with Accommodation Bridge behind serving the footpath from Bailey Brooks Lane

Dr Stephen Clements retired from the partnership in 1982, but continued to serve until 1987. He left a practice which had changed from one with rudimentary facilities to a modern Medical Centre with branch surgeries covering a wide area.

Dr Alan Sutton joined the practice in 1969 and, when Dr Clements moved to Ashton, he moved into the house adjoining the surgery known as "The Doctor's". Dr Clements became Senior Partner of an enlarged practice when the three practices of Roade, Hanslope and Blisworth merged in 1965, followed by Dr Sutton when he became the Senior Partner of the practice, succeeding Dr Clements. Dr Sutton had been a member of Roade Parish Council (including a period as Chairman) and he retired as partner in 2003 after 34 years service. Dr Hillyer is now the Senior Partner.

GPs of the Roade/ Blisworth/ Hanslope Surgeries at the retirement of Dr Stephen Clements
Left to right - Front row: Drs Stephen Clements, John Sorrell
Centre row: Drs Derek Bull, Alan Sutton, Tony Hillier
Back row: Drs Lyn Moore, Ian Daplyn

The Surgery in 1996 where the original outline of the Fox and Hounds can still be seen within the extension

The surgery before a car park was added in the 1980s

At Roade Medical Centre there are qualified and ancillary staff supporting the partners. The practice has been extended yet again to include Grange Park, where a purpose-built medical centre provides facilities for residents living in that area.

Staff at Roade Medical Centre in the mid 1990s

Left to right: Joanna Edmunds, Pamela Peers, Elizabeth Dyke, Melanie Stephens, Diana Farebrother, Angela Speight, Dr Alison Otto

The present (single) Charity traces its roots back to the seventeenth and eighteenth centuries.

CHAPTER 7

Charities

ROADE FEOFFEE AND CHIVALL CHARITY

The cottages in the 1920s when two of the four (far right) were quite low and thatched. By 1928 they had been rebuilt.

The present (single) Charity traces its roots back to the seventeenth and eighteenth centuries.

Documents deposited with the Northamptonshire Record Office show that the Feoffee Charity was established in the late sixteenth or early seventeenth century. Land belonging to Antony Ward, and in the occupation of his ancestor (Wylliam Wardes) in the time of Queen Elizabeth I, was transferred to nine trustees (or feoffees) by an indenture dated 5th July 1633. The feoffees also owned the Town House and four acres of land. In the early 18th Century the income of the estate was used to help inhabitants who fell into accidental misfortune, and later to buy coal and to subscribe to the Northampton Infirmary. After inclosure the feoffees received 10 acres at the Plain, near Blisworth Road, adjoining land belonging to the Chivall Charity. The Town House stood at the junction between Ashton Road and what is now

Memorial Green, and it was converted into tenements for six to eight tenants and the premises were described as Poverty Yard. The tenements were later reduced to four, and the feoffees rebuilt these cottages in 1927. This is the origin of the Memorial Green Cottages of today which have been progressively updated since the 1960s.

The Chivall's Charity came from a widowed mother and her daughter who conveyed 14 acres of land to trustees in 1708. The income was to be dispersed to the poor. In Ashton a similar trust from the two women with capital worth fifty pounds in the 1750s appears to have been lost due to the insolvency of a borrower. Progressively, the Charity Commissioners have become more and more involved in the reorganisation of the two Roade Charities and they were amalgamated in 1956. The latest scheme is dated July 1997 with the two charities forming one trust – Roade Feoffee and Chivall Charity. The Charity is to apply its income, after meeting the cost of maintenance of the four cottages and the costs of administration, towards the relief of any residents of "the Ancient Parish of Roade who are in conditions of need, hardship or distress".

Roade Feoffee and Chivall Charity Cottages (centre), c.1930

ROADE AND QUINTON OLD FOLKS FUND

Walter Judkins

In 1962, the death of a single Roade householder, whose body lay undiscovered for several days, caused a wave of concern in the village. At a meeting held in the old British Legion hut on Church End, the Old Folks Fund and Tote were set up as a means of raising money and keeping in weekly touch with the elderly.

The Tote was started in 1963 by a small committee, chaired by Walter Judkins, and an army of collectors. One of its first aims was to buy a large property and convert it into a residential home for the elderly, but this was later abandoned due to costs.

By 1965 the Fund was providing completely free annual holidays for the over 65s of Roade; a novel enough event at the time to merit the Mayor of Southsea turning out to meet the coaches. In more recent years escalating costs meant that the Fund could not provide free holidays, but it has continued to organise accommodation and subsidised transport for annual holidays.

The Fund also distributed a parcel of groceries (including poultry in the early days) to pensioners each Christmas. The sick were not forgotten and received Easter gifts.

Seniors outing

Outing to Southsea

The Christmas parcels and Easter gifts, largely funded by the Tote, continue to be distributed. Elderly villagers who have moved into residential care homes are remembered; they are given a plant at Easter and receive toiletries at Christmas.

The Christmas Concert, held at the British Legion Club, remains a very popular evening with the locals. Everyone enjoys the excellent fish and chip supper followed by entertainment and dancing to a live band.

In recent years the committee has organised half day coach trips to Coton Manor, Bicester Village, Rutland Water and a boat trip round Oxford. Occasional concerts have also been arranged starring the Abbey Minstrels, at Roade Sports College, and Roade Choir and Orchestra, at The Ex-Servicemen's Club.

The village owes a huge debt of thanks to the organisers and the many collectors who walk the village to collect 'The Tote' in all weathers.

Seniors outing, 1983

Seniors outing, 1996

Charles Rennie Mackintosh designed furniture and

decorations for Candida Cottage.

CHAPTER 8

Houses and Cottages - Past and Present

There are many interesting and attractive houses and cottages to be found in Roade. These are just a few of them, together with some which no longer exist.

Four cottages formerly at the far end of Bretts Lane

The four cottages with Ken Oakey (Left) and Stan Tapp (Right) in foreground, c.1930

The two cottages which were later replaced by Nos 27 and 29 Bretts Lane

These cottages, 2 each side of Bretts Lane, formerly belonged to the Grafton Estate. They were demolished in the 1960s and replaced by two farm cottages on the north side and a row of garages on the south side. The garages have now also been demolished and replaced by 10 Bretts Lane.

Tilecote House, Hartwell Road

Tilecote House, Hartwell Road

Tilecote House, standing at the corner of Bretts Lane and Hartwell Road, was designed by Edward Swiffen Harris (1841-1924) of Stony Stratford, an eminent architect in this area in the late Victorian period specialising in schools and church design. Tilecote was built between 1894 and 1897 for Dr Walter Ryan with 7 bedrooms and 3 reception rooms. He held his surgery in a small outbuilding in the garden. The house is little changed externally from its original design, although the coach house has been converted and is in separate ownership together with the neighbouring small thatched cottage which also formerly belonged to Tilecote.

The Coach House after conversion

27 Hartwell Road with pear tree covering the front wall

29 Hartwell Road covered with roses in 1949

27/29 Hartwell Road - Pear Tree House

Pear Tree House was formerly two cottages. It is dated 1717 but was altered and extended in the 19th century. Elizabeth Higgins (née Jackson) was born in No 27 in 1858 and later lived there with her husband, William Higgins, who managed the farm opposite. Their daughter and her family (including Syd and Derek Humphrey) lived in No 29. Later the two cottages were combined and for many years Syd Humphrey lived in the former No 27, using No 29 for his collections.

28 Hartwell Road -
Holly House old and new

Holly House, a former Grafton Estate cottage, was a condemned building when it was purchased by John Whatton and his fiancée Anne in 1955. John demolished the building and a new Holly House was built, with John himself completing all the internal carpentry. It was finished in time for occupation after Anne and John were married in November 1958.

Above: Old Holly House seen from Pear Tree House, c.1950

Left: New Holly House, 1958

The Homestead,
1 Ashton Road and 3 Ashton Road

The Homestead dates from the 17th century. At the time of inclosure in 1819 it was a house and malt-house belonging to Robert Cave, a farmer and the second largest landowner in the village after the Duke of Grafton. By 1853 it had become a small-holding extending to about 4 acres, taking in what is now the adjacent PSL car park. Prior to the Grafton Estate map of c1720, an extension had been added to infill the gap next to No 3 Ashton Rd, the eastern end of which was bought for £30 and converted to a Methodist chapel, opened in 1852, and known

The Homestead, 1 Ashton Road, in 1985

locally as the Malting Chapel. At one time, a maltings was added to the back of The Homestead and is now the dining room, but may by this time have been moved to the site of the chapel. When the new Methodist Church was built in Hartwell Rd in 1875, the chapel was allowed to deteriorate and was eventually demolished.

Samuel Tew, the local Coal Dealer, bought the property in 1853, the business passing to his son, also Samuel, who died in 1924. The property was gradually divided up, but the house and cottage belonged to the extended Tew family until 1972.

When she died in 1972, Elsie May Tew owned the two cottages now known as No 3 Ashton Road, together with the adjoining former Methodist chapel and the field which is now the PSL car park.

The Methodist Chapel was demolished and, in August 1972, the eastern 8ft of the gap this had created was gifted to The Homestead. The field was bought by PSL for their new car park and the cottages gradually fell into disrepair. In 1988 the cottages were purchased by the owners of 1 Ashton Road, the land boundaries modified and then sold for demolition and rebuilding by Alan Humphrey of Roade as a single, extended house, in a similar style (the house is now 8ft longer than the original).

Rear of No 3 Ashton Road, early 1980's

No 3 Ashton Road during reconstruction, c.1988

4 Memorial Green - Pound Cottage

4 Memorial Green dates from the late 17th century although the interior was reconstructed in the 1990s. Next to the cottage (on the Ashton side) was the former village 'pound', an enclosure where stray animals were kept until released on payment of a fine.

Elizabeth Higgins and May Kightley outside 'The Pound', c.1905

Right: The Pound during renovations, c.1990

Left: Pound Cottage and Crimble Cottage, 1998

14 and 16 Memorial Green

14 Memorial Green also dates from the late 17th century but was altered in the 19th century. The old roof timbers could be seen during rethatching. At the Grafton Estate Sale in 1913 it was bought by Mr A F Lenton together with a large garden and orchard and the premises on the corner of Hartwell Road, all previously occupied by Mr T J Gray, blacksmith and wheelwright (see top photograph on page 28 in Around Old Roade). No 16 Memorial Green was built for Mr Lenton and was sold to Mr R H Cotching in 1928. The Lenton family continued to live in No 14 until 1986.

14 Memorial Green being rethatched in 1981

14, Right and 16, Left, Memorial Green

Cottages formerly on the site of Three Ways in Hartwell Road

These cottages belonged to the Grafton Estate until 1913. They were demolished in the mid 20th century.

Top: The cottages (left) early 1900s

Right: The cottages, c.1930

1 Hartwell Road – The Old Manor House

1 Hartwell Road was the grandest of the Roade houses owned by the Grafton Estate and was described in a mid 18th century survey as *'a good stone house ...now much out of repair'*. 19th century tenants included the Revd. William Butlin and his farmer grandson, William Edward Butlin. The Grafton Estate continued to own the house until 1913, when it was bought by Mr C F Alsop, a solicitor, and named 'Fairlawn'. In 1933 'Fairlawn' became the home of Mrs Locke and her daughters, Gladys and Peggy (a respected music teacher). After the Locke sisters died (in the early 1960s) the house was bought and renamed by Mr Derek Tarry, who sold the land on which Manor Close and 3 Hartwell Road were built.

The Old Manor House in 1998

20 Hartwell Rd - Stone House

Built in 1880 by local builder George Goodridge as his own family home, Stone House was erected on land forming part of Cock Close which was later worked as a quarry. His spinster daughter, Louisa, lived here until her death in 1953. The house remains substantially 'as built' and has been owned by only 5 families in 130 years.

Stone House, Hartwell Road

Far left: The Chaplin's cottage with old cemetery gate (right)

Left: Mrs Emily Chaplin outside the cottage

Cottage formerly on site of 2 The Green

This former Grafton Estate cottage was once the home of the Chaplin family. The present No 2 The Green was built next to it around 1963 and the old cottage was then pulled down. The cemetery gate was moved when Manor Close was built in the 1960s.

Frederick Gray's wife, Eva, outside the cottage

4 The Green - Corner Cottage

This cottage was the home of the Gray family for many years. It was one of two neighbouring former Grafton Estate cottages bought by Mr Frederick Gray, wheelwright, carpenter and undertaker and son of Mr T J Gray. The smaller cottage became a blacksmith's workshop but was demolished after No 6 The Green had been built on the site of the old yard in 1990. The equipment from the workshop is now in the Abington Museum in Northampton.

Gray's Yard

Front of former manse

1 The Leys - The Old Manse

In 1738, a year after the Baptist Church was built, accounts refer to the *'building and repairing of the dwelling-house'* - the manse between the Church and The Leys. The accounts include payments for ale at various stages of the building work. Around 1860, the top room of the manse was used for the making of hair-nets, which were then the fashion among young ladies. After the death of the last pastor, Ray Lineham, in 1993, the manse was sold and it is now a private house.

Rear of manse backing onto graveyard

Cottages formerly opposite No 2 The Leys

Between the old vicarage drive and The Leys stood a row of one-up/one-down Victorian cottages. These were demolished by Pianoforte Supplies Ltd in the early 1960s and the site now forms part of the Bowls Club grounds.

The now-demolished cottages (upper left) in The Leys in 1960

1. The Home Guard outside the vicarage

2. Old vicarage front

3. Girl Guides at the vicarage, late 1940s

4. The vicarage showing site of present bowling green

The Old Vicarage - formerly in The Leys

An imposing vicarage was built in The Leys in 1844 and was the scene of many village festivals and activities. During World War II the stables were used as a fire station, the vicarage was used as the headquarters of the Home Guard and over two tons of food were stored in the cellar and attics. After five years, sugar and tea stored in the attics in ordinary wrappings were found to be in perfect condition. Because of heavy maintenance costs, the old vicarage had to be replaced by a smaller one in Hartwell Road (Highfield, built for Mr C F Alsop). The old vicarage was sold to Pianoforte Supplies Ltd in 1953, subsequently demolished and replaced by the Bowls Club.

8 Church End - Church House

8 Church End is thought to date from the 17th century or earlier, originally thatched and probably extended upwards in the 18th century. The barn backing onto the churchyard is believed to be older than the house. The earliest maps of the village show that the property once included a strip of land behind the house bordering the churchyard. In 1951 the house (then called Myrtle Cottage) was bought by Job Sturgess, who had been its tenant for many years.

Job Sturgess in the garden, 1948

Church House

Premises in front of the house (left), when occupied by F J Hails, baker

38 High Street - Uplands

Uplands formerly belonged to the Grafton Estate. In the 18th and 19th centuries, the tenants were farmers and bakers. The house was sold by the Estate in 1913 but the last tenant (baker F J Hails) remained there until 1916. It was then bought by Mr J E (Ted) Harris, who put a date stone 'JEH 1916' above the front door. Mr Harris ran a garage and car hire business. Since the Harris family left the village in 1937, the house has been a private residence. The old buildings in front of the house were demolished when the High Street was widened in the 1960s.

Uplands

The cottages before conversion

Candida Cottage after conversion with Mrs Bassett-Lowke (no hat) on the front door step and Mr Bassett-Lowke on the steps of the loggia

39 High Street - Candida Cottage

In 1914 model manufacturer Mr W J Bassett-Lowke bought the pair of dilapidated cottages in Roade which were to be converted into *'a really ideal country home'* (according to an article in the Ideal Home Magazine in 1920). The conversion was carried out during and after the First World War and in the process it was discovered that the two cottages had originally been one. The Bassett-Lowkes called the cottage after one of George Bernard Shaw's plays, 'Candida'. A letter from Shaw to the Bassett-Lowkes regarding a visit to Candida Cottage was in the possession of a subsequent owner of the cottage, Frederick Bailey, in the 1970s but unfortunately the letter cannot now be traced. In 1917 Mr and Mrs Bassett-Lowke received a book of Shaw's plays as a wedding present from the architect Charles Rennie Mackintosh and his wife.

Dining room

Letter from Charles Rennie Mackintosh

Dining room

Dining room with trolley beside fireplace

Bedroom

Bedroom showing door to balcony and wardrobe

The Bassett-Lowkes lived at 78 Derngate, Northampton, and used Candida Cottage as their country retreat. Charles Rennie Mackintosh designed furniture and decorations (including stencils) for Candida Cottage as well as for 78 Derngate and some of the 'Candida Cottage furniture' can be seen at Brighton Museum and Art Gallery. Mackintosh was responsible for the remodelling of 78 Derngate and, although there is no evidence that he advised on the actual conversion of Candida Cottage, the loggia, doors and windows are reminiscent of his style. It is possible that Alexander Ellis Anderson, a local architect of Scottish origin, was consulted.

Mr Bassett-Lowke himself had a keen interest in modern architecture and design, and had worked in an architect's office before joining the family firm. He played a very important part in the design of all his homes. For example, he sent Mackintosh a drawing of a trolley (or 'service table') to be used at Candida Cottage. The final version can be seen beside the fireplace in the dining room. Bassett-Lowke is also thought to have designed the bedroom furniture. The wardrobe is now in the Cecil Higgins Art Gallery and Museum, Bedford.

Jean Hudson outside the cottage in 1955

The cottage later became known as St Michael's Apiary, because the then owner, Frederick Bailey, kept bees there. The Davis family only became aware of its history in 1984, after having lived there for 5 years, and have renamed it Candida Cottage.

The loggia, 1984

Fred Bailey holding cup

Marie-Helene Davis, 1984

Station Road - railway cottages formerly on site of Pianoforte Supplies Ltd 'bottom shop'

Pianoforte Supplies Ltd bought these cottages from the railway authorities and demolished them in the 1960s in order to build the 'bottom shop' adjoining the recreation field. Glenys Parry, whose father was a signalman, was born in one of the cottages and lived there as a small child. Glenys married Neil Kinnock (now Baron Kinnock), the Labour Leader from 1983–92, and herself became a successful politician and MEP.

Station Road cottages, c.1900

Roade's first Council Houses - The Leys

In 1919 ten council houses were built on the east side of The Leys. There were no houses opposite them at that time. Until 1937 they were the only council houses in Roade.

Helen House (L) and council houses, c.1930

Prefabs - formerly on site of Stephenson Court, Hyde Close

The 'prefabs' were built in Hyde Close in 1947/48. These were intended as a temporary solution to the post-war housing shortage and were expected to have a life of five to ten years. In fact they lasted for over forty years until they were demolished to make way for Stephenson Court.

Prefabs

Prefabs being demolished in 1991

Grafton Road and Hoe Way in the 1950s - not a car to be seen

Start of Churchcroft Estate, 1966

Churchcroft is one of several large housing developments built in the 1960s. This photograph was taken from the end of the path leading past St Mary's Church from Church End.

CHAPTER 9

Businesses and Shops

INTRODUCTION

The development of the different modes of transport during the Victorian era resulted in significant population growth in Roade. New businesses were formed and shops needed to support the growing and increasingly mobile population. Roade has more of these than most villages, several having been here for many years. Here are some examples.

Pianoforte Supplies Limited

Pianoforte Supplies Limited (PSL) was established in London by Cyril Cripps in 1919 to manufacture and supply components for pianos (as its name suggests).

The company soon needed larger premises and Cyril Cripps moved his business to Roade in 1923 taking over the factory building of the defunct Simplex Polish Works at the end of The Leys. Pedal feet, strings and hinges continued to be manufactured for the piano trade until the end of the 1970s. The old name was retained despite changes in activities over the years.

Simplex Polish Works, c1920

The aftermath of the fire

Aerial View of factory, 1936

In November 1933 there was a disastrous fire which destroyed the old Simplex Works. The Fire Brigade had great difficulty putting out the blaze due to an inadequate supply of water. The factory was rebuilt in 1934, still with its entrance at the end of The Leys.

Prior to the Second World War, manufacturing had expanded into making metal components for the motor industry and the work force increased to some 400.

Social Club Outing, 1939

Left to right: Cyril and Amy Cripps with Gilbert & Mrs Tarry and Ray Smart, 1936

Opening of the Canteen in 1938

A modern canteen and social centre was built which also provided amenities for the villagers at large. Later it was the venue for a "Workers' Playtime" which was broadcast on the BBC Home Service. Older readers will remember these variety programmes from factories on war work round the country.

During the war, manufacturing concentrated on production for the war effort, including smoke floats and flares, as well as parts for aircraft and motor vehicles. Cyril Cripps

Staff at the Opening Dinner

Aerial view of factory, 1947

Toolroom Lads, 1950

From left: back row: Bunny Hill, Don Abbot, Cyril Curtis, Johnny O'Dell, Tom Salter, Vic Johnson, Cecil Swannell, Roger Fox

Middle row: Ron Hayward, Ron Botwood, Tony Bellam, Jim Davies, Ted Merriman

Front row: Alan Rose, Peter King, Albert Holding, John Atterbury, Tom Pike, Bernard Webster

was awarded the MBE for the war work. After the war, production of components for motor cars was expanded and, in addition to those for the piano trade, hinges were made for motor vehicles and aircraft. Examples were bonnet hinges for motor cars and for luggage compartments on motor coaches. Regular deliveries had been made to London before the war and also to Coventry, Oxford, Birmingham and Luton. Later, the transport department was separated from

the manufacturing business and deliveries were made in Chaplin's lorries whose expanding business is on the Stratford Road. Ultimately customers collected goods from the factory using their own contractors, which included Chaplins.

By 1953 employees numbered some 800, many of whom were brought into Roade from Northampton and surrounding villages by coaches or buses hired by the company for the purpose.

Polishing Shop, 1948

Hinge Shop, 1948

The premises were steadily expanded by building on the adjacent land, and as more suitable buildings came into use, the old 1934 buildings were progressively vacated.

The last of these to be used was the Hinge Shop, above the old Press Shop at the end of The Leys. This was vacated in 1980 when the manufacture of piano strings was discontinued and hinge making was transferred to newer premises within the main factory. The major part of the output was now components for the motor industry which was itself changing. Hub caps, grills and similar external trim items were now being changed from chromium plated metal to plastic. With the increase in pressed metal bodies, cars ceased to have door frames as a load bearing part of their structure. The financial climate also compelled mergers of car and commercial vehicle companies, which all became even more assemblers of components made by sub-contractors. Eventually most of the old names disappeared except as marques of the combined entities. Employment at PSL peaked at 1,800 early in the 1960s

Some diversification was attempted in the 1960s, for example into manufacturing spin dryers, but these proved so robust and long lasting that demand dropped as no replacements were required! Eventually PSL

Bending Dept, 1948

Plating Shop, 1948

adapted by utilising a former Ministry of Production building in Croft Lane and acquiring an existing business in Wellesbourne, Warwickshire. Both these sites concentrated on plastic extrusion and injection moulding, principally for the motor industry.

The main factory was still involved in metal components, suitably painted, powder coated, plated, anodised or polished. As the requirements for these decreased, so more production lines were introduced to manufacture combinations of metal and plastic, such as bumpers, door frames and decorative trim. By 1980, numbers had fallen to some 700 due to increasing automation and the decreased need for metal components. The first redundancies had occurred in the previous decade to adapt the size of the work force to the new requirements. Competition from Japan, and later from Eastern Europe and even South America, meant business was becoming more and more difficult for UK-based manufacturers. Numbers steadily decreased until, by the end of 2007, there were less than 150 employees and since then they have fallen further with many of the remaining employees being on short time.

Over many years PSL and Cyril Cripps supported a number of charitable and educational activities including the local secondary school (later to become a Comprehensive and Sports College). A swimming pool was provided there which is also used by the Primary School as well as by the community outside school hours. A Chair of Metallurgy was founded at Nottingham University and the Cripps Centre at the Northampton General Hospital, as well as Cripps House in Roade. Cyril and his son Humphrey (who succeeded him in the early 1970s) supported numerous other educational establishments, including buildings for Colleges in Cambridge and the new High School

on the Newport Pagnell Road in Hardingstone, Northampton. Cyril Cripps was knighted for work in connection with the restoration of the Cathedral in Peterborough. His son was also knighted after serving as High Sheriff of Northamptonshire in 1985.

Sir Cyril and Lady Cripps at Buckingham Palace in 1971

Sir Humphrey and Lady Dorothea Cripps with their daughter Eleanor and son Edward at the Palace in 1989

Walkerpack Ltd with PSL Buildings on far side of the railway

Walkerpack Ltd, 1982

Walkerpack Ltd

The roughly triangular site between the railway, the A508, and the footpath to Gravel Walk, was an open field before inclosure in 1818. In 1773 Benjamin Marriott of Roade bequeathed the five acres of 'open common and commonable fields' to his wife Mary and then to her son, who split or sold it off. At one time it was owned by nine different people. The parcels of land were at various times called Mill Piece, Barker's Close (adjoining the station), Station Field, Gridiron Piece, Clarkes Close and Glebe Land.

Local names of owners include Marriott, Paggett, Butlin, Winters, Cave, Howes, Jackson, Molcher, Curtis and Walker. Their occupations include Gentleman, Grocer, Beer House Keeper, Yeoman, Maltster, and Farmer, so it probably continued in agricultural or horticultural use throughout the period up to the 1960s. The Swan Inn, in the south-east corner of the plot (also known as the Swan brewhouse), was mentioned as newly-erected in an Abstract of Title of A.C.B. Praed dated July 1878. The inn is believed to have been decommissioned in 1961.

The land and Swan Inn were acquired from Phipps Brewery by a removals, packing and haulage enterprise operating from the old Tivoli Cinema in Far Cotton, Northampton, owned by the Walker family, and established at Roade in 1967.

Units were built there to house its activities, and the former Swan Inn was transferred to the general manager.

Industrial use continued, staff numbers rising to well over a hundred, until Walkers moved to Brackmills in the 1990s, and the land was sold to developers in the early 2000s. The units were demolished in 2007, and current plans are to site a housing estate there.

T. Roddis Ltd

Thomas Roddis, the son of a farmer from Ashton Lodge, established a contracting business in Roade at the turn of the last century, undertaking steam ploughing, threshing and similar work for local farms. One of his traction engines was involved in an accident so spectacular that at least two postcards depicting it were produced for sale and the following report appeared in a local paper:

A Northampton-built Allchin steam lorry, thought to be with Thomas Roddis and a member of his staff standing in front, c.1920

'*How did it get into such an extraordinary position is the question that at once suggests itself.*

Yesterday afternoon quite a crowd of children and others from neighbouring villages stood upon the bridge gazing at the great iron horse as it lay cold and still with the water swirling round its bent and twisted parts.

The engine, which belongs to Mr Roddis of Roade, was being driven on Tuesday towards Grafton Regis, two men being in charge, and when on the bridge it was decided to fill the water tank of the engine.

The roadway is about 10 feet above the level of the water and, at this point, the river is between 10 and 12 yards broad and three feet deep in the middle.

The driver proceeded to back the engine towards the edge of the brickwork of the bridge, along which is fixed a wooden railing for the safety of persons crossing.'

The story goes on to describe how one man climbed down the bank to place the engine's pipe in the stream but found it would not reach.

'*The driver backed the engine a little nearer the edge of the bridge. The result was disastrous, for the impetus given to the engine was too*

great. The tender squashed into the railing and broke it down and one of the great rear wheels of the engine went over the brickwork.

The man directly beneath looking after the pipe made a frantic rush underneath the arch of the bridge and the driver reversed the engine in a moment. But it was too late for in a second the wheel and tender of the engine hung over the river and the huge machine lurched sideways.'

In 1900, Thomas Roddis built an office (now the front part of 2 Hartwell Road) with works behind. The business was incorporated around 1914 as T.Roddis Ltd and became a large local employer. The firm went out of business in the early 1920s and the office was converted into a dwelling around 1930.

A postcard depicting the accident on 9th October 1906, on the bridge over the River Tove, just before Tollgate Cottage on the A508 near the turning to Alderton

P. Chaplin & Sons

Following service in World War I, Percy Chaplin started in business as a coal merchant delivering to customers in Roade and other local villages. He bought his first motor lorry in the early 1930s.

At first he operated from the former Roddis Steam Engine site on the Hartwell Road and then moved to Slipe Farm on the Stratford Road which he bought in the 1940s. During the Second World War, he farmed and continued to run the coal business. At various times he served as an emergency ambulance driver and at the Observer Post situated on the Blisworth Road. It was during this time that he 'house moved' a number of evacuee families from Coventry and London.

Later, and following service in WWII, his sons, Tom and Frank, joined their father in the business and were then later joined by their brother Fred.

Gradually the enterprise grew, the coal business was sold and they concentrated on general haulage which continues to this day. The business is currently run by Percy's surviving sons, Frank and Fred and by grandson Tom.

Frank Chaplin

Chaplin's vehicles with their Drivers including Keith Horne, Wilf Gulliver and John Burnell

Major Arthur Mallock in a Mk 2 "U2" at Mill Cottage, The Grove, January 1959

Mallock Racing

Major Arthur Mallock started the company in 1958, producing cars from his garage, before the company moved to Olney. The model name "U2" was based on the famous Charles Atlas saying, but changed to 'You too can have a Racing Car like mine'. The cars are front-engined, space-frame-chassis Sports Racing cars. Arthur's expertise in suspension geometry, chassis rigidity and sound engineering lives on and the cars offer good value and exciting racing. More than 300 have been produced and sold worldwide. Cars and their owners came from all over the world to Silverstone in 2008 to celebrate 50 years of this remarkable marque.

Arthur Mallock died in 1993 and, together with his wife Kay, is buried in Roade. His son, Richard, now runs the locally-based company with help from his wife, Sue, and son, Charles.

Roade Quarries

There have been several quarries in the parish, but no stone merchants are listed in Roade before the 1880s, although small scale quarrying presumably took place at an earlier date.

In 1862 the Northampton Mercury quoted the Revd. Maze W. Gregory, vicar of Roade, speaking at the Architectural Society of Northampton, *'In most places under the soil is a thin stratum of stone, which they call "pendle", and, beneath another layer of earth, a thicker rock, which is very good for building purposes, and, when burnt, makes good lime. It is extensively used for mending the road, but it has this disadvantage, that after it has been exposed to a frost, it falls to pieces, and becomes mud, or more properly speaking, cement. I once saw, on the Hartwell Road, several heaps of broken stone, after a hard frost, breaking up and becoming mud even before they were laid down. But in this state, also, it is very useful and is much used; and I believe the inside of most walls are worked with pure Road dirt (I don't know whether to spell Roade with or without an e), and the outside only with regular mortar. It makes capital walls for hovels, too, when plastered over wattles; but for road purposes it is particularly bad; indeed, the village locomotion in winter should be called "wading" rather than walking'.*

One quarry was on the Hartwell Road, south east of Bretts Lane; after it closed Percy Ayers kept chickens there.

Another quarry was sited on the west side of Hartwell Road. Millions of tons of limestone were excavated from this quarry where Horace Parish later tended his orchard and ran his poultry farm. Both sites were subsequently bought by Pianoforte Supplies Ltd: they used the old

The Bretts Lane quarry was in the field at the lower centre of the photo

Top: The Hartwell Road quarry in bottom right hand corner, c. mid 1970s
Bottom: The Hartwell Road quarry as it is today

Hartwell Road quarry as a site in which to dump effluent and plating residue. This ceased in the late 1970s when the surface was grassed. The level is now substantially above the gardens of neighbouring houses. Nearby the remains of two lime-kilns were found when the foundations for a factory building were dug in 1936.

The largest and most important business was that developed by the Sturgess family, who began as jobbing builders in the mid 1800s. Between the 1890s and the First World War the firm did building work and supplied materials to a range of local authorities, estates, farmers, pubs, schools and chapels amongst others, mostly within a ten-mile radius of Roade, but also in places served by the London & North Western Railway between Wolverton and Rugby. The L.N.W.R. itself was their largest single customer until about 1910, after which they appeared to lose the business entirely. In the same period they also carried out work for the Stratford & Midland Junction Railway. Another

The Stratford Road quarry c1990 at lower left of photo

customer, the Simplex Polish Co., located at the end of The Leys, went out of business in the 1920s.

Between the two World Wars, when the firm was run by William David Sturgess, it appears to have concentrated mainly on quarrying limestone in the quarry south of the village, on the east side of Stratford Road. A shrewd business man, William worked the quarry in three directions; towards the railway, the road and the canal, so that he would have the choice of three methods of transport. He built his own lime-kiln and employed about thirty men, with Gerald Reed as Foreman (he later kept the Swan Inn). He laid his own single line railway, the 'Jubilee Track', to connect with the Stratford and Midland Junction Railway line, where the limestone was transferred from his wagons to railway trucks and sent to the Hunsbury Hill ironworks. Most of the stone was carried by road, but an order from London Zoo, to supply large pieces of stone, weighing not less than 5cwt each, to make one of the rockeries, was sent by canal.

In the early 1920s some of the stone was sold for road metalling or house building and the softer stone was burnt in a kiln at the quarry to make lime for cement and mortar manufacture. During the General Strike in 1926, transport and foundries, like many other branches of industry, were paralysed and smaller firms could not bear the loss. Hunsbury Hill ironworks closed and other Northamptonshire furnaces were too far away to provide an alternative market.

A Rugby firm, F. Palmer & Son (Quarry) Ltd, worked limestone at the Stratford Road quarry in the 1950s and was among the suppliers of stone to the M1 motorway. This quarry, also acquired by PSL, was used for many years for the disposal of plating and other effluent after the Hartwell Road site, behind Stone House, had been filled. This was discontinued a few years ago and the site is now a haven for wildlife.

THE CO-OPERATIVE SOCIETY IN ROADE

In June 1916 the Northampton Co-operative Society bought a piece of land in Hartwell Road to build a shop and a house. Building was completed in 1919 and the store opened in 1920. It immediately proved to be very popular and it was noted *'that trade rose to £100 per week within a month'*.

Mr Walter Hudson was appointed manager of the branch in 1944 and moved to the house with his family in 1945. At that time the grocery trade was very different to that we are used to today. There was no 'self service'; thoughtful customers would call for their weekly order already written up in their own 'order book'. There was little impulse buying in those post-war days.

An early photograph soon after the opening in 1920

The Staff at Roade Co-op, 1946

Left to right: Walter Hudson, Rene Gray (Simpson), George Bailey, Ellen Watson, Edna Barratt (Hillyard), Betty Shipman (Henshaw)

Goods were delivered in bulk from a central warehouse in Northampton and weighed and individually bagged by the staff in one of the rear rooms of the shop – flour, sugar, butter, dried fruits etc. were all handled in this way. Cheese came in large round cakes, two cakes in a wooden crate and bacon was delivered in complete sides, boned and sliced on the premises to customer's requirements.

In 1945 there was a staff of six and a delivery boy. Each week one assistant set out by cycle to 'canvass' for orders in surrounding villages – Courteenhall, Stoke Bruerne, Shutlanger,

Grafton Regis, Ashton and Hartwell. Those orders were prepared and delivered to customers, initially by horse and dray and later by motor van. In 1953 a large 'mobile shop' based in a purpose built garage at the rear of the shop toured those villages. The first driver of the van was Mr George Bailey of Ashton.

Showing the demolition of Roade Co-op Shop. The Garage for the Mobile Shop can be seen at the rear.

The extended house after the demolition of the shop

Milk and bread were delivered directly to customers by vans from Northampton and were usually paid for by 'checks' purchased from the shop. A mobile butchery shop called at the village twice each week. The Society withdrew the service in 1987, but it is continued privately to this day by Peter Clarke who started working with the Co-op in 1974.

In later years changes in trading and the enormous growth of the national supermarket chains led to a decline of business and the Co-op ceased trading in Roade in the early 1970s. Subsequently the shop was used by Graham Laidler for his 'Shop Fittings' business. Later the shop was demolished and the house enlarged. The garage at the rear of the shop was also demolished and replaced with a new house.

Peter Clarke with his mobile shop

HOW THE HIGH STREET SHOPS HAVE CHANGED OVER THE YEARS

The shop front under construction

'Roade Fayre' Shop with car park

In the 1960s part of a row of cottages at the upper end of the High Street was demolished and the site used to develop an entrance for a shop and car park. The premises, developed by Mr Newman, a grocer from Towcester, became the village's first self-service store.

The opening of the new self service shop which also shows the narrow High Street at the time

Later, Civil's, a Northampton-based supermarket chain, took over the business. They were followed by two further proprietors and trading continued until 1997. The building also contained a small hairdressing salon next to the shop entrance. A flat was later built above the shop which linked through to the cottage bedrooms with access via steps from the car park. In 1989, Peter Doddington and Ros Cowap, trading as WVS (Welcome Vending Service) took over the hairdressing premises and later, in 1997, the shop. They continued trading from there until 2003 when the business was sold. Things have now turned full circle; the shop has been demolished and two new stone cottages built on the site.

1. Civils Store in its heyday with a window display designed to be noticed!
2. Welcome Vending Service premises after the self-service shop had closed
3. WVS and vehicles
4. Cottages back on the site again

Mr Alan Allen with the billboard he used to display outside his DIY yard. This photograph was taken when he gave a talk to Roade Local History Society

Allens DIY Centre

Mr Allen bought Elm Farm in the 1956. He did building work locally and people started to call to see whether he would let them have a bucket of sand or gravel to save them a journey to Northampton. Over the next twenty years, from this very small beginning, a large DIY enterprise was established. In the 1980s the business was sold to Butterfields, a company from Luton. They wanted to expand the business but were unable to get planning permission so the business was closed, the land sold and subsequently used for new housing. A new library was built on an adjacent plot owned by Northamptonshire County Council.

"Allens of Roade" in the High Street

According to trade directories, Mrs Sarah Fisher was already a shop-keeper by 1901 and her name last appeared in 1936. By about 1940, Mrs Gardner and her daughter Eveline (Eva) were running the shop from the front room of their cottage in Yew Tree Terrace. A bell was triggered when the door was opened and one of them came through from the back of the house to serve. They sold a wide variety of goods ranging from general provisions and toys, to pins and needles, sweets and toiletries. It closed in the early sixties.

Mrs Sarah Fisher's shop at 35 High Street, c.1920

Mrs Butler's former Shop, 2009

"Uplyme Cottage", 19 High Street, is opposite Church End and was once a shop run by Mrs Butler. The stone steps leading to the door are still in place but the shop window to the right has been filled in. The shop was definitely open during the Second World War and sold various items including rationed food to customers who registered with them. It is not known exactly when the business started or when it finished.

The Howard family moved to Roade from London during the Second World War. They lived in this cottage with an adjoining shop which had previously been run by a Mr Warren. The Howard family continued to use the end room of the cottage as a shop and later it was used by Ray Parish for his Greengrocery business.

Shop at 28 High Street opposite The Leys, c1900 complete with tin baths for the many who needed them

In the 1920s Vic Turner and his family lived at 9 High Street and he ran his butchery business in the shop, now the Post Office, facing the High Street. By request, orders were delivered to customers by 'butcher's bicycle' – a large basket was mounted in a rack at the front. Later Tim Turner joined his father in the business and for a time he leased a second shop in the Ridings. After Tim's retirement in the 1980s, a butchery business continued for some time until the property was bought by Mrs Osborne in the 1990s. After modifications, Mrs Osborne transferred the Post Office business from her house, 'Hillcrest', on the opposite side of the High Street.

Tim Turner standing outside his butcher's shop

Roade Post Office has relocated at least five times since the mid 19th century. The first Post Office, established in 1854, was run by Mr William Hands who was also a grocer and honey dealer. Mr Alfred J Martin moved the Post Office Counter to 'Hillcrest' in 1939. The business continued in these premises until Mrs Osborne transferred the Post Office across the High Street to the former Butcher's shop in the 1990s.

"Hillcrest" housed the sub-Post Office from 1939 until the 1990s

Roade. High Street

Roade. High Street

Valentines Series   45648

A forgotten Grocery shop

This recently-discovered photograph shows that a substantial shop/house existed in the late nineteenth century between the White Hart and Hillcrest. Two very different activities – grocery and tailoring – seem to have been carried on side by side. It appears from an old Trade Directory that at some stage the village post office also operated from here. A small remnant of the building can still be seen – the doorstep remains in place and is now at the base of the wall of the Roade House Car Park, adjacent to the pavement on the High Street.

Site of the former Grocery shop, 2009

Millie Henman in the doorway of Gossages shop, c.1940

At the beginning of the 1900s Mr William Martin ran his butcher's shop from these premises, with an adjoining Slaughter House. The entrance of the Slaughter House is on the extreme right of the photo. (There was apparently no window in the building but the upper half of the door could be opened for light and air.) By the 1930s Mr Gossage had a Newsagent business here. Later Jim Howard took over the business on this site until he moved to a larger shop in the 1950s. For a short time Derek Tarry sold groceries in the shop and later the premises were taken over by "Richardsons' Commissions" who established a Betting Shop. It is now Jackson Grundy's Estate Agent office.

Jackson Grundy's office with one door blocked up and the two ground floor rooms combined

The former bake house is reached by the alley between the Newsagent and A C Construction Ltd and is situated in the yard behind the parade of shops in South View.

A recent photograph of one of Roade's old bake houses

Jim Howard's Newsagent in 1982

Shop at 4 High Street in early 1900s

Although the exact date the shop opened is not known, by 1903 Frederick Davis was trading from here as a grocer. Some years later Mr Percy Ayers, a baker, moved into the property. In addition to the bakery he also ran the Post Office from the shop. Bread was prepared and baked in the brick building which still stands in the Bakers Yard. The bakery was later sold to Bill West who sold bread and cakes in the shop and also made deliveries round the village. In the 1950s Jim Howard moved there with his already established Newsagent business from the present Jackson Grundy Office. The shop is now run by Tushar Patel and his family who have expanded the business to include lottery tickets, wines and spirits and general stores.

By 1903, Mr John Gregory was already trading from these premises as a boot maker and sub-postmaster. He also had a further job as Clerk to the Burial Board. The shop later became a butcher's and Mr Goode acquired the business in 1934. He was succeeded by his son Roger. Between them, they ran the shop for over sixty years. In more recent times it has been a fishing tackle shop, but is now an office for A C Construction Ltd.

Mr Gregory's shop in early 1900s

Roger Goode left, with Jim Sinfield in the doorway of the Butcher's shop

"The Roade Boot Shop" in South View

Mr and Mrs Mason standing outside their Boot Shop c.1940 where they offered "High Class Repairs" The shop was in front of Manor Farm and adjacent to the row of terraced houses in South View. Mr Mason also put on film shows for the village children in the room above the shop. After the war they moved into Warwick House and continued the shoe repair business from their new address. The old cobblers shop was subsequently demolished.

Following the conversion of two houses in South View, there are now four shops in the terrace. The original corner shop, shown in the photo as Goode's butchers shop, has been joined by a draper's and a pharmacy with a hairdresser's above.

South View shops today

The advent of local owners would have given rise to the
need for local service and fuel supplies.

CHAPTER 10

Garages

Among the earliest vehicles operating in Roade were undoubtedly Thomas Roddis's steam traction engines in the late 19th century. Gradually, petrol-driven cars would have been seen in, and passing through, Roade. The advent of local owners would have given rise to the need for local service and fuel supplies. After the First World War, one of the village's two blacksmiths set up as an agricultural and motor engineer and J. E. Harris opened a car hire service. A second garage was opened by W. J. Brazier later in the decade and in the 1930s Roade had three such businesses as well as a haulage contractor (Horace Parish).

Registration document for Bert Dunkley's Jowett *(NRO)*

Harry Sturgess in an American Locomobile "48" Touring of 1914

The Dunkley family in their Jowett outside Elm Farm, late 1920s

We believe Harry Sturgess had a motor agency at one time, although this is likely to have been in Northampton. Other early owners include Mr W.A. Stimpson and Mr C.F. Alsop, a solicitor. The next locally-owned car we can trace is Bert Dunkley's 1920s 7hp Jowett.

Cycle Agents

John Cave Butlin had a bicycle shop in a building in front of Manor Farm from around 1906 until he died in March 1924. By this time Alfred Jesse Martin was also in business as a cycle agent. Garage-owner John (Jack) Frederick Martin had become a cycle agent by 1931. His uncle, Alfred, was the Postmaster.

John Martin

A postcard, showing the High Street and Harris's garage on the left, 1930s

Harris's Garage

Mr J E (Ted) Harris had a motor garage and car hire business located in the High Street opposite Yew Tree Cottage. He traded from buildings (later demolished) in front of his house, now called Uplands. He inserted a stone, JEH 1916, over the front door to commemorate his purchase. He sold the house in 1937.

Main's Garage

This was located in the once-named Wrights Yard, off the access to Candida Cottage from the High Street. It was started by George Main. He used to sell oil to villagers who had no electricity and had to rely on oil lamps, even though mains power came to Roade in 1929. He lived in the bungalow on the north side of the old Police House. He is remembered as having a glossy moustache and wearing plus fours with a large-checked jacket.

High Street Garage invoice of 1961, when petrol was 4/6d per gallon (5p per litre!)

Jack Reed worked at Roade Main Garages in Stratford Road and left in the late fifties to take over George Main's garage, possibly after his death. The name may have been changed to High Street Garage at this time. The garage closed in the eighties. He bought the site of Jack Martin's garage in Stratford Road and built the current premises.

The access to Main's Garage in the High Sreet, is to the left of the photograph alongside Yew Tree Cottage, c.1967

The entrance viewed from the opposite direction, c.1967

Martin's Garage, Stratford Road, 1960

Martin's Garage

John (Jack) Frederick Martin, a local boy born in 1900, was the son of William Martin, who had a butcher's shop in the High Street (currently Jackson Grundy's office). After completing his apprenticeship with Rolls Royce in Waterlooville, Hampshire, Jack returned to Roade in the early 1920s. He set up business on a piece of land where the Shell petrol station is today. The early building was made of corrugated iron and extended piecemeal as the need arose. As motoring was in its infancy, Jack also traded in paraffin and the sale and repair of new and second-hand bicycles, in addition to selling National Benzole petrol and repairing cars. He also made crystal radios and charged up accumulators and batteries in a lean-to, wired to a panel of flashing lights arrayed along one wall. He ran a car hire business with a black Ford V8 Pilot car, often used for weddings. *(see wedding photo of C Patrick & M Lane on page162)*. Another activity was the sale of cigarettes. He kept small spare parts in identical, unlabelled Oxo boxes with no note of the

contents. This could mean a long wait for customers until the right tin was found! Trading was a seven-day activity with occasional breaks to go on train excursions from Roade Station to the seaside. He was an agent for Royal Enfield Motor Cycles and, at one time, was sponsored by them to race their motor cycles on grass.

In the 1960s, a spark from a welding torch started a fire and the complex was burnt down. Fortunately, the three fire engines which attended managed to prevent the petrol supply igniting. Jack escaped relatively unharmed but sadly, Scamp, the guard dog died at his post. Despite all this, Jack set up a garden shed on the site and carried on selling petrol as usual. He later sold his land to Walkerpack. They subsequently sold it on to Jack Reed who had a brick garage built with servicing facilities, a retail showroom for cars and petrol sales. The new garage was called Reeds Motor Co.

Below: Reed's Garage, Stratford Road, 1980s

Roade Service Station and Costcutter

Jack Reed's son, Chris, ran Reeds Motor Co, the Service Station in Stratford Road and, as well as selling second-hand cars, took on the Maserati agency. The economic climate was probably instrumental in its demise.

After several owners, and the conversion of the showroom to a Spar shop, the business was taken over by the current owners in 1998. The Costcutter franchise replaced Spar and was developed into a mini supermarket to support the retail petrol sales.

Main Road Garage

Tommy Cooper was born in 1890 and, at the age of 20, emigrated from Puxley, near Deanshanger, to the USA. He stayed several years in America, and then returned to Potterspury, then back to America again before finally settling in Roade with his American wife, Edna, and their two daughters in

1929. Tom started Main Road Garage on the A508, near the railway bridge, and employed 8 people. He also ran a taxi and bus service, with Edna driving the taxi. He later sold the bus enterprise to Charlie Griffin. Tom died in 1957/8.

Tommy Cooper and bus on his forecourt in 1947

Aerial view of Roade Main Garage in 1980

The garage business was bought by Derek Tarry and the name changed to Roade Main Garages Ltd. He opened a general grocery shop in what was described as the "car show room" and had a Fish 'n' Chip shop built on the edge of the property, in The Ridings.

On 20th December 1960, Bill Hemming bought the business from Derek Tarry, and his wife took over the shop. The name was changed from Main Road Garages Ltd to Roade Main Garage. At that time there were three mechanics: Bert Baker, Sam Wickham and Ken Nash. Bill died in 1979 and Mrs Hemming ran the Garage until their son, Jack, took over in 1983. The petrol pumps were converted to self-service in 1988 and administered from the shop.

Roade Main Garage, 1982

Installing the 5000 gallon petrol tank in 1990

Jack Hemming, 1990

Roade Main Garage, 1990

Demolition of No 2 Stratford Road, once owned by greengrocer, Mr Denton

The workshop was later extended and No. 2 Stratford Road was purchased. The house was demolished in 1998 to provide better access and more parking for the garage. Activities were expanded into sales of second-hand cars some 15 years ago, in addition to repairs and servicing. The petrol pumps on the forecourt were closed in November 2007, and the garage now employs a staff of six.

The village carrier continued to transport items by horse and cart until the mid 20th Century.

CHAPTER 11

Cabs and Carriers

Horse-drawn cabs going to and from the station were a familiar sight in Roade in Victorian and Edwardian times. The village carrier continued to transport items by horse and cart until the mid 20th century, although by then parcels could be delivered by the United Counties bus.

Mr Jeff Butler in his brougham, c.1900

The George Hotel, c.1900

Butler & Son, Cab Proprietors

'Butler & Son, cab proprietors', appear in trade directories from 1903 to 1914. They operated from the George Hotel, where cabs were 'always ready' for travellers arriving at the station. The photograph above shows Mr Butler junior in his brougham. His father appears in one of the photographs of the George Hotel in Pubs and Inns (Chapter 13).

Carrier Martin, 1900

Village Carriers

The villages around Northampton used to have 'carriers' who would transport items to and from the town by horse and cart. This photograph came from 'The George' and is labelled 'Carrier Martin 1900'. It is probably of Stephen Martin, a carrier from Stoke Bruerne, who would have passed through Roade on his way to Northampton.

Carriers from Northampton would also pass through Roade and around 1864 a *'melancholy accident'* occurred there *'to a man named Frost, in the employ of Messrs. Higgins, of the George Hotel, in this town [Northampton].*

Frost had been sent out with a van to deliver a quantity of wine and, on passing over the railway bridge at Roade, the horse shied and Frost was pitched over the bridge, falling a depth of sixty feet. He was immediately picked up and brought to the Infirmary where he remains, but slight hopes being entertained of his recovery'. The vicar of Roade, Maze Gregory, kept a newspaper cutting about the accident. He noted that the depth was actually sixteen feet and the carrier had recovered.

The Roade carriers are mentioned in 19th and early 20th century trade directories. For example, in 1885 Joseph Skears of the White Hart ran a service on Monday, Wednesday, Thursday and Saturday to Northampton and on Tuesday to Towcester. Later, Job Sturgess recalled *'Mr Skears ...with his carriers van with old*

Toby, a marvellous horse, standing over 17 hands with great flat feet which you could hear flop, flop, flop, coming up the hill ... & turning up "White Hart" yard at full speed when there would be 2 of Skears' boys waiting to take him out and give him a hot mash, always mixed with a quart of old ale. He was supposed to have done the journey from the White Hart at Cotton End, Northampton, in 20 minutes.' From 1898 until the mid 20th century the carrier went to Northampton twice a week on market days - Wednesday and Saturday. The service was run mainly by members of the Skears and Abbott families until around 1936, when Horace Parish was the carrier. Horace's main occupation was poultry farming and he also had a stall in the old Fish Market in Northampton. By 1940 Horace's brother Arthur had succeeded him as the village carrier.

Arthur Parish's house, c.1950

Ray Parish remembers his uncle Arthur well and sometimes helped him. Arthur lived in a cottage in the High Street, to the right of the shop which is now occupied by Jackson Grundy. The cottage has now been incorporated into the Roade House. Arthur went to Northampton on Wednesdays and Saturdays, leaving Roade about 9 o'clock and arriving at Northampton about 10 o'clock. He would put up at the Bell Hotel in Bridge Street, where he would feed and stable his horse. Anyone with a parcel to go to Roade would come to the Bell and put it on Arthur's cart - 2d a small package, 4d a big one. Kinghams of Abington Street, for instance, would send groceries to customers in Roade. At about 3 o'clock Arthur would emerge from the pub, somewhat the worse for wear, and doze in the cart while the horse took him home. When he got to Roade he would deliver the parcels or get Ray or another boy to do it for him. Ray used to enjoy delivering the parcels and could drive a horse and cart from the age of 10. During the rest of the week, Arthur, or his young helpers, delivered to local villages. As well as orders from the Roade Co-op, he sometimes made deliveries for the undertaker and Ray would be disconcerted to see a coffin in the cart. At the same time Arthur sold vegetables and fish, which he collected from Roade station once a week. He also kept pigs behind his cottage. He died in 1951.

Mrs Bowdidge outside her cottage in Ivor Terrace, some time between the Wars

United Counties Carrier Service

Mrs Bowdidge's cottage in Ivor Terrace (at the top of the High Street, near the A508) was used as a collection point between the Wars for parcels transported by the local bus company, United Counties. Parcels taken to the old bus station in Derngate, Northampton, could be delivered to villages on a bus route. Mrs Bowdidge was well placed for the agency as she lived by the bus stop.

During the rail construction, around 900 men and boys were employed day and night in 12 hour shifts.

CHAPTER 12

Railways

'Our railway' was originally developed mainly for leisure traffic, with goods being carried once the power of the locomotives was improved.

It was built with 2 tracks (1 Up [to London] and 1 Down) by the London - Birmingham Railway Co. The cutting excavations took four years and were completed in 1838. It was considered such a difficult feat of civil engineering that parts of the work were personally supervised by Robert Stephenson.

The original cutting was 1½ miles long and 65 feet (c. 20 metres) at its deepest. During the construction, around 900 men and boys were employed day and night in 12 hour shifts, with only Sundays off. Accommodation was in huts at the top of the cutting, with no furniture, and beds of straw. They were located over the bridge at the end of Bailey Brooks Lane, consequently known as Accommodation Bridge

passengers from Northampton to be picked up and set down.

An unfortunate result of the construction of the cutting was that it acted as a deep drain and the underground flow of water to the village was disrupted. Wells that once contained water a few feet from the surface now needed to be sunk many feet down. The aqueduct constructed in 1837 over the cutting, just north of Accommodation Bridge, obviously did little to avoid the problem.

In 1846, the London and North Western Railway Company took over the LBR and the first 'proper' Roade Station was built in 1851. The lines were duplicated during 1875 - 1882 and the cutting was increased in depth on the east side to bring the new Northampton Line down to level ground as it passed Milton Malsor.

'The Northampton loop line under construction, 1881
(NRO ref P3038)

The landslip in Roade Cutting, 1890

The total cost was around £5 million, which was an astronomical figure in those days, equivalent to several billion pounds at today's prices. At the time, it was the biggest civil engineering project built by 'Free Labour' in Great Britain. Even so, only basic station accommodation existed initially to enable stage-coach

However, following a major landslip in this deeper cutting in 1890, it was rebuilt using brick facings and finally was reinforced with 100 vertical steel supports with cross girders. The completed construction was known as 'The Birdcage'.

Aerial view of the PSL factory and the two adjoining sidings, 1950

Roade sidings in 1948

ROADE CUTTING, SEPTEMBER, 1904.

This photograph of Roade Cutting, looking north, in September 1904, carries the insignia of the London & North Western Railway Company in the bottom left corner

Further amalgamation of railway companies led to the London Midland and Scottish Railway Company taking over the LNWR in 1923. The station was subsequently rebuilt by the new company and, apart from the Ticket Office, remained substantially unaltered until closure.

Two sidings came off the eastern side of the main line with a large area between. This area was designated as the coal yard, allowing coal to be unloaded and stored ready for collection by the coal merchants. Post World War II, these coal merchants were Chaplins of Roade (now Chaplins Transport) and Wiggins & Co. Ltd. Industrial and agricultural equipment was also unloaded in these sidings, with Pianoforte Supplies using them for the receipt and despatch of goods.

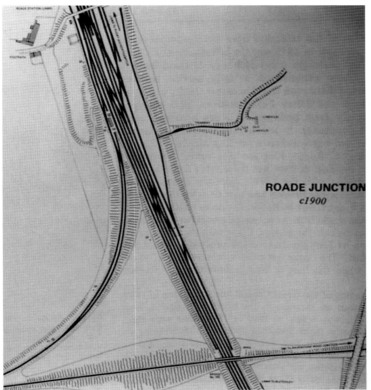

The junction of the LNWR and SMJ railways in 1900, showing the tramway from the limestone pits at upper right and The Swan pub and the footbridge at the top left

In the early years there was a tramway running from the Limestone pits near Ashton Road. This allowed the tramway wagons to reach the railway via a wooden support and tip their load into the railway trucks.

A branch of the Stratford-on-Avon and Midland Junction Railway (SMJ) ran from Stratford-on-Avon, via Towcester and Stoke Bruerne, to join the Northampton – Bedford line at Ravenstone Wood Junction, just north of Olney. It passed over the main lines via a girder bridge, built in 1891, at the south end of Roade station. The route passed under the Ashton Road, close to the PSL water tower, and under Hartwell Road between the Fox Covert estate and Castellana House, just outside the village. The line became defunct in 1958 and was finally dismantled in 1964. The old SMJ was known locally as 'The Scratter' and also, at various times, somewhat affectionately, as the 'Slow, Miserable and Jolty', the 'Linger and Die' and the 'Bread and Herring'. It is not known if the word Scratter has any connection with a traditional cider apple mashing machine of the same name.

A goods train headed towards the SMJ line at the Junction, Aug 1890. The wooden loading ramp from the tramway can be seen at upper left

Construction of the extra bay for the SMJ line at Roade Station, c.1890

This rail ticket from Roade to Northampton was issued on 31st July 1948 and cost 5p!

Station Master Percy Stephens & staff, 1944. He was Station Master at Roade from 1940 to 1960
From left: Albert Walker, Mike Connolly, Mrs Una Stephens, Harrison Whitlock, Percy Stephens, John Pell and Dorothy Campion

As road traffic increased, a footpath over the A508 bridge became sorely needed. Trying to cross the bridge was described as like 'playing Russian Roulette'. The current footbridge was added in 1953.

The opening of the A508 footbridge, July 1953, attended by, from left:
RN Saunders, Arnold Bailey, Alderman WD Sturgess and Alderman JD Brown
The Primary School Headmaster, Mr Harper, is standing on the roadway

The Booking Office as rebuilt in 1957
(Graham Onley)

It was quite usual for small parcels to be delivered in the Guards coach at the rear of a passenger train. These were then put onto the platform for transferring to the Parcels Office by the Porter to await collection.

On Sunday 6th September 1964, the last train stopped at Roade and the station closed the next day – part of the 'Beeching Axe' - and was completely demolished down to track level. The only remaining buildings are the Stationmaster's house, now a private dwelling, and the Booking Hall/Parcels Storeroom which is now a workshop.

A goods train on the mainline Down line in Roade Cutting, 23rd June 1962

Left: Leaving Roade Station,1932. The now-demolished Station Road cottages are to the right, *(L. Hanson)*

Bottom left: A goods train about to enter 'The Birdcage' on the Up line from Northampton, 1963

Bottom right: A goods train on the Up line passing through Roade Station from Northampton, 1962 *(L Hanson)*

The electrification of the West Coast Main Line started in 1959 and came through Roade in 1966. The height of many bridges had to be increased to accommodate the wires and overhead structures.

The reconstruction of Ashton Road bridge, 1961

Roade Station following electrification

Roade Station prior to electrification, 1956

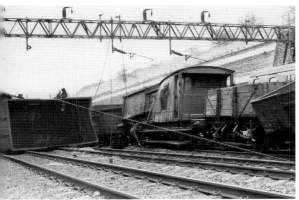

Collision in Roade Cutting, 31st December 1969

One of the first bridges to be raised was the Ashton Road bridge over the railway, on the southern edge of the parish. The existing roadway and base were removed, the two supports each side of the railway were increased in height, then new reinforced concrete beams laid and the road surface re-laid. The girder bridge which had carried the SMJ Railway over the main lines was also removed. The bridge carrying the footpath over the lines at the southern end of the Station site was increased in height. At the Courteenhall end of the cutting, an even bigger civil engineering job was the removal of the cross beams of 'The Birdcage' over the Northampton lines with the height of the vertical supports increased by a few inches and the cross beams replaced.

On the West Coast Main Line through Roade, 1980

CHAPTER 13

Pubs and Inns

THE COCK

The Cock, c.1910

The Cock Hotel, c.1920

The Cock, 1982

In the garden are a sundial and three seats in memory of popular landlord Bill Reid, his wife Jackie and daughter Claire 'friends of us all'

All three were killed in an accident on the M1 in 1991

The Cock's date of foundation is unknown. The building appears on the earliest map of the village (c.1720) and was a farm as well as an inn. It has been suggested that the name could relate to cock fights. In 1816 meetings regarding the inclosure of the open fields were held 'at the house of Mr William Paggett known by the Sign of the Cock'. By the time the inclosure was completed, William had died and his heiress, Elizabeth Paggett, owned 84 acres in the parish. This included a large area south of the inn on the west side of Hartwell Road including Cock Close (now consisting of the quarry site and Stone House) and Cock Field (now occupied by the PSL factory).

In the 1850s Job Ashby's licence included a clause barring 'men and women of notoriously bad fame, or dissolute boys and girls'. The number of pubs in the village had grown

ROADE, NORTHAMPTONSHIRE.

PARTICULARS AND CONDITIONS OF SALE
OF
18 FREEHOLD HOUSES,
WITH THE GARDENS AND APPURTENANCES,
AND
A CLOSE OF ARABLE LAND,
CONTAINING 3a. 1r. 0p,
SITUATE IN THE VILLAGE OF ROADE,
Which will be Sold by Auction, by
MR. W. J. PEIRCE,
ON
FRIDAY, THE 17TH DAY OF MAY, 1872,
AT
THE COCK INN, ROADE,
AT FOUR O'CLOCK IN THE AFTERNOON, SUBJECT TO THE CONDITIONS HEREINAFTER SET FORTH.

PARTICULARS.

Particulars of sale held at the Cock Inn, 17 May 1872

following the building of the railway and in 1862 the vicar lamented that there were then 'six to 669 people'.

On 17 May 1872 an auction was held at the Cock of property which had belonged to the late Joseph Campion. Lot 3 is now 2 The Leys and Lot 4 is now 4 - 10 The Leys.

In 1924 the Cock was praised as 'a place where a working man can get a good dinner for two shillings' [10p]. Now the pub is open all day and is still a popular place to meet, eat and celebrate.

The White Hart, c.1900 (NRO PBP78)

The White Hart Inn, c.1924 (NRO PBP 945)

THE WHITE HART - (NOW THE ROADE HOUSE)

This was a popular pub in the 19th and early 20th centuries. A redoubtable Victorian landlady was Mrs Skears, who had been known to seize a man by the back of his collar and eject him from the pub. She never opened on a Sunday and was the last to be buried in St. Mary's churchyard before it closed in 1894.

In 1949, a darts team was formed which proved to be very successful and quickly rose to league A. The village cricket and football clubs also used the pub in the early 1950s. It later closed and was virtually derelict by the mid 1970s, when it was transformed into a high quality restaurant, The Roade House.

Group outing from the White Hart, c.1950

THE ROADE HOUSE RESTAURANT AND HOTEL

In the mid 1970s the old White Hart pub was converted into a restaurant. The third owners since its re-opening, Chris and Sue Kewley, bought what was then called 'The Roadhouse', in October 1983. In 1997 they incorporated the adjoining cottage to create ten guest bedrooms. The Roade House has built up a strong local reputation, has been listed in the Good Food Guide since 1985, and also appears in the Michelin, Hardens and AA Restaurant Guides.

Chris & Susan Kewley receiving AA Rosette, 5 December 1985

Chris & Susan Kewley outside The Roade House

Entrance to the Roade House Restaurant and Hotel, 2009

THE FOX AND HOUNDS

The Fox and Hounds stood facing the junction of the A508 and what is now Hyde Road, a back road to Blisworth which gave access to navvies' huts along the railway cutting. It seems to have been founded by the 1840s, perhaps slightly earlier, probably to exploit extra demand created by the navvies. It lasted to the 1920s, when it was converted, first into a private house then a doctor's surgery and residence.

On 23 December 1861, a drunken scuffle took place at the pub which resulted in the manslaughter of a young carpenter, George Marriott. He was struck on the forehead with a stick by a tinker named Booth and sent home in a wheelbarrow. Unfortunately, the

The Fox and Hounds, c.1900

front of his skull was unusually thin and he died about 8 days later. The incident prompted a sermon by the vicar, the Revd. Maze Gregory, based on the text *'The voice of thy brother's blood crieth unto me from the ground.'* Copies of the sermon were sent to every house in the village.

The George, c.1890

THE GEORGE

Originally named after the railway engineer, Robert Stephenson, who supervised work on Roade cutting, The George opened in 1839, a year after the London to Birmingham Railway. In the period up to the creation of Northampton Loop Line in 1882, it must have been very busy, offering horses and cabs for hire, and meals as well as drinks to travellers awaiting trains and coaches. The name was changed to the George by 1844 for unknown reasons. The pub closed at Christmas 2007 and was demolished in 2009.

George Hotel, Mr Butler senior is in the foreground, c.1910

The George just before demolition, 2009

A note attached to the safety rails of the demolished building: "Thanks for the memories R.I.P. THE GEORGE"

THE SWAN

The building which was once the Swan Inn is behind the Costcutter shop next to the footpath between the PSL factory on Ashton Road and the A508. It seems to have been built in the 1870s, as it was described as a "newly erected beerhouse" in an abstract of title dated 6 July 1878. It was an old-fashioned house, drinks being drawn in the tap room and carried on trays to customers in the parlour. It was very popular with railway and factory workers, and regulars sometimes went on holiday outings together. It closed in 1959 and is now known as The Swannings and used as an office.

The Swan Inn, 1970

Swan Inn outing, 1950

Gentlemen -
Left to Right:
Harrison Whitlock, Richard Dyke (Sen), 'Darkie' Ashby, George Denny, Richard Dyke (Jun), Sid Green, Gerald Reed (Pub Landlord), Jim Whitlock, Charlie Harrison, Eric Smith, Douglas White

Ladies: Minnie Whitlock, Jane Dyke, Mary Whitlock, Mrs Ashby, Mrs Denny

THE NEW INN (WOODLEYS FARM)

This was an important coaching inn on the turnpike road (now the A508) near the Blisworth turn and the landlords were also farmers. At least one 19th century landlord, William Barker, was also a well known horse dealer. He had stabling for 100 horses on the opposite side of the road from the inn and provided horses for London cab drivers. The inn is mentioned by Charles Dickens, who stayed in it on his travels. With the decline in the coaching trade, the inn reverted to farming as part of Courteenhall Estate. The premises are now a Day Nursery.

Woodleys

Vine Cottage

OTHERS

In 2009 three other licensed premises were operating in Roade - the Ex-Servicemen's Club, Roade Football Club and Roade Bowls Club. In earlier centuries there were various beer retailers and alehouses in the village, one of which was in or near Vine Cottage. Vine Cottage was one of several in White Hart Yard next to what is now The Roade House, but it was demolished around 1938. Along with a number of other cottages in the village it fell foul of new fire regulations and was condemned because it had only one outer door. Some of the families who lived in the condemned cottages moved to new houses in Hyde Road.

The 1831 inventory of a shopkeeper named George Pacey, who owned the buildings which are now 4, 6 and 10 The Leys, shows that he brewed and possibly also sold beer. No 4 The Leys was once a pub or alehouse and its cellar had a ramp down which barrels could be rolled. Unfortunately, little is known about it, as it does not appear in the Trade Directories, but it is thought to have been called the Pear Tree.

CHAPTER 14

Sport

Sport has always played a big part in the life of the village. Some Clubs no longer exist, but others have taken their place.

CRICKET

Early cricket in Roade is not well documented. There is a reference to Dr Ryan (1853 – 1927) having a team which used to play on a ground *'near the quarry on the Stratford Road'*. Others recall playing in the area near to the present site of the Roade Sports College and others in a field off the Hartwell Road, near the SMJ line (the Scratter).

A Roade Cricket Team, c.1920

Left to Right - Back row: George 'Darkie' Ashby, unknown, Jack Hillyard, Ted Curtis, Harry Curtis, unknown, Gerald Reed

Middle row: unknown, unknown, Percy Chaplin

Front row: unknown, Charlie Chaplin, the rest are unknown

Roade Cricket Club

Roade Cricket Club was formed in the 1940s and matches were played in the field next to the current PSL car park on the Ashton Road. Sometime after the Second World War, Mr Cyril Cripps, the owner of

The opening match, 6th May 1956

The two teams and, in the centre, Mr Cyril Cripps with Dennis Brookes, Northamptonshire C.C. Captain, on his left, and Mr Harold Stafferton, President of Roade C.C. on his right

PSL, presented the idea of establishing a designated cricket ground. The project went ahead and an excellent cricket ground was laid out with a pavilion built on the site, alongside Northampton Road. Situated as it was, with the Parish Church on one side and open fields on the other, it was undoubtedly a perfect setting for a cricket ground and the envy of many other clubs. The opening match, on the 6th May 1956, was played between Roade Cricket Club and a Northants County Team. The Northants XI was captained by George Tribe and the Roade XI by Jock Livingston. Frank Johnson, the Roade Captain at that time, handed over the captaincy to Livingston for the match. Both George Tribe and Jock Livingston were Australian Internationals. The match was also a George Tribe Benefit Match – and he was caught, out for a duck!

The Teams list for the opening match autographed by the Northamptonshire players

Frank Johnson, a long time member of Roade Cricket Club and captain for several years

With their splendid new ground, the Roade Cricket Club went on to considerable success playing in the North Bucks League, the Northampton Town League, and the Northants County League.

Roade Cricket Team (with visitors), 1950

Left to right - Back row: a visiting umpire, Fred Blincow, Dave Curtis, Frank Johnson (Umpire), Pete Stevens, Walter Denny, George Johnson, Denis Hillyard

Front row: a visiting batsman, Stan Robinson, Arthur Bird, Ted Curtis, Harry Curtis, Len Davies, a visiting batsman

Roade Cricket Club, 1952

Left to right - Back row: Jim Davies, Walter Denny, Clarence Puttnam, Les Beeby, John Neesham

Front row: Geoff Tasker, Brian Wardale, Harry Curtis, Peter Tompkins, Clem Donoughue, Richard Johnson

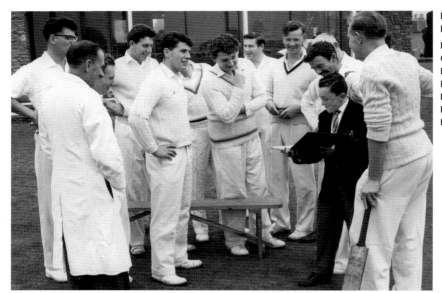

Roade Cricket Club, North Bucks League Champions, 1961

Left to right: Frank Johnson, George Johnson (Umpire), Dave Trueman, Roy Herbert, Peter James, Don Abbott, Doug Walker, Vic Hooper, Roy Chapman, Alvin Barby, Ken John

Roade Cricket Club, 1965

Left to right - Back row: Doug Walker, Keith Nixon, Ben Middleton, Keith Threlfall, Alvin Barby, Roger Heighway, John Jarrett, Fergal Collins

Middle row: John Capel, Kevin Essam, unknown, Bert Bream, Charles Wall, John Neesham, Peter James, Alan Hopper, Francis Hill

Front row: Don Abbott, Sir Cyril Cripps, Frank Johnson

Roade Cricket Team, July 1971

Left to right – Back row: Ray Clements, Keith Nixon, John Capel, Frank Johnson, Terry Allen, Les Cole, Ted Curtis

Front row: Keith Threlfall, Paul Thompson, Ben Middleton, Doug Walker, R.Jones

David Capel

David Capel, born at Roade, was a member of the Roade Cricket Club. David displayed great talent and went on to play first class cricket for Northamptonshire C.C.C. from 1981 and he represented England in 15 test matches and 23 One Day Internationals. Since 2006, David has been Head Coach and First Team Manager for Northamptonshire County Cricket Club.

David Capel awarded his County Cap, June 1986

David in action in the Bi-Centennial Test in Sydney, 1988

Roade Cricket Club, 12 July 1994

Photograph taken before the start of David Capel's Testimonial Match against a Northamptonshire County X1 as part of his 'Benefit Year', 1994

Left to right - Back row: Paul Moffatt, Steve Cole, Nigel Griffiths, Mick Scott-Evans (umpire), Paul Mason, Ben Baxter, Michael Howkins, Mick Deacon, Peter Lyons, Stuart Moffatt, Chris Denton (umpire), Dale Johnson

Front row: Simon Turner, Liam Collins, Brian Curtis (Chairman), Dave Clarke, Andrew Capel, Keith Threlfall

Demolition of the Cricket Pavilion, April 2008

Unfortunately, in later years, interest in cricket declined and the field has been allowed to deteriorate. The pavilion was demolished in 2008.

FOOTBALL

Although early history is very sketchy, there are records of regular friendly matches between local villages as far back as 1898. Many records of the period 1911 to 1920 were lost, probably because of the upheavals of the First World War.

There are records of a Roade Team playing in the Central Village League from 1920 and during that decade there were two teams – Roade Albions and Roade Simplex.

Apparently the two teams amalgamated in the 1930s and by the 1948/9 season the Albion suffix was discarded.

Roade Albion Football Team, early 1900s

The names on the back of this photograph are unclear, but include Dunkley, Pell, Hillyard, Martin, Chaplin, Gray, Parish, Hobson, Walker and Flood

FRANCIS, PASSMORE, H. PARISH, F. ATACK, C. CHAPLIN, R.L. WALKER, V. TURNER, MR ALEXANDER

G. DOUGLAS, WESTLEY, A.J. MARTIN, W. WALKER

A. PARISH, ROBERT E. TAIT, E. BAILEY

Roade Football Team, 1920/1

Left to right - Back row: George Green, Fred Walker, Jack Hillyard, Horace Parish, Vic Turner, Horace Pankurst
Middle row: Harry Smith, Walt Richardson, Charlie Chaplin, Bill Walker, Harry Poole
Front row: Percy Chaplin, Harry Curtis, Sid Whitlock, Arthur Parish, Flip Hobson

Roade Football Club

From the little extant documentation and memory, a local public house was the headquarters for the Club and it had many different bases – in the 1920s the Cock Inn, 1940/50s the George and the White Hart. From the 1960s the Club has had its own premises off Hyde Road.

Initially, the Club played in the Northants Central Village League, moving to the North Bucks League then to the South Midlands League. In the early 1970s they returned to the North Bucks League and finally to the Northants Central Combination. Over the years the Club has been very successful winning League titles and various competition cups.

Football Team Honours since 1953

North Bucks Division 2 South Winners 1953/4

North Bucks Premier Cup Winners 1974/5

North Bucks Premier League Champions 1991/2

North Bucks Intermediate Cup Winners 1995/6

North Bucks Premier Cup Winners 1996/7, 1998/9

F.G. Watts Sunday Division 2 Champions 1999/2000

North Bucks Premier Cup Winners 2001/2

North Bucks Division 2 Cup Winners 2002/3

Roade Football Club, c.1950

Left to right - Back row: W. Walker, C. Wilson, M. Connolly, I. Oakey, J. Howard, P. Howard, G. Shipman, F. Johnson, D. Hillyard, B. Dearsley, E. Barnes

Middle row: A. Taylor, T. Barnes, R. Denny, C. Cripps, H. Stafferton, W. Barnes, J. Atterbury, A. Prior

Front row: Don Curtis, J. Poole, P. Paxton, E. Thomason

Roade Football Team

Runners-up in the Central Village League 1946/47

The match was against Brafield and played at Blisworth

The players -

Left to right: E. Walker, J. Whitlock, Dave Curtis, F. Johnson, F. Swain, P. Paxton, W. Denny (receiving cup), P. Walker, F. Roberts, A. Bird, T. Smith, W. Barnes

Roade Football Club – North Bucks League, 1965/66

Left to right - Back row: M. Connolly, K. Horne, P. Gibbs, A. Hopper, P. Duberry, G. Green, T. Cooke, B. Gardener

Front row: R. White, B. Webb, J. Capel, T. Shakespeare, K. Barby

Roade F.C., 1996/97 season

Left to right - Back row: J. Blackmar, G. Warren, J. Ratcliffe, L. Hillyard, D. Brett, B. Duff, M. Whitmare, R. Hawes, A. Hillyard

Middle row: R. Frost, R. Paxton, M. Powell, N. Powell, D. Johnson, M. Spring, N. Howard, L. Cowley, K. Parfitt, S. Brown, M. Connolly, Don Curtis.

Front row: Dave Curtis, I. Fall, C. Shakespeare, P. Andrews, S. Maddison, D. Eustace, S. Moffatt, D. Hillyard, M. Chambers

Mike Connolly working as
Groundsman, 1990

Mike Connolly (centre), Chairman of Central Northants Football Combination, 1966-7

Mike Connolly

Mike 'lived' football and was involved with Roade Club for 50 years, first as a player, then secretary, treasurer, linesman and 'half-time tea maker'! In 1966-7 he was appointed chairman of the Central Northants Football Combination.

After retirement from his work at British Rail, he took on the post of chief groundsman at the Club and assisted with the running of Friday Nights Bingo. Locally, he was affectionately known as 'Mr Roade Football Club' and the entrance road to the Club from Hyde Road is named 'Connolly Way' in his honour. Mike died in 2001.

Junior Football

Roade Junior Football Team, 1949

Left to right -
Back row: Brian Sturgess, Paddy Howard, Keith Faulkner, Eddie Dennis, Keith Thomas, Tony Curtis, Richard Johnson

Middle row: Peter Tompkins, Bernard Webster, Bernard Donoughue, Clarence Puttnam, Brian Wardale, John Collins

Front row: Alan King, Charlie Wilson

Roade under 11 Cup Final Team, 2002

Left to right - Back row: C. Summerlin, J. Newman, S. Haase, J. Whitlock, P. Preece, J. Tapp
Front row: J. Stevens, G. Owen, T. Sedgley, R. South.

BOWLS
Lawn Bowls

The Pianoforte Supplies Ltd Bowling Club was founded as the Simplex Bowling Club in 1957 when Sir Cyril Cripps provided land in the grounds of the former vicarage. The old croquet lawn made a good base for the initial three-rink Green. At 5 shillings joining fee and the same as the annual subscription, it attracted 23 members for the opening.

The Honours boards in the Clubhouse pay testimony to the standard of play achieved over the years by both the men's and ladies' teams at County level.

PSL bowls ladies

Left to right: Mrs Dolly Bland, Mrs Dorothy Piper, Mrs Nancy Gilson, Mrs Eva Warren, Mrs Iris Anderson and Mrs Kathleen Grose

PSL Bowls Club, 1968

1. Chris Haggett 2. Frank Johnson 3. Tyrell Barnes 4. Ron Botwood 5. Jim Collins 6. Frank Clarke 7. Maurice Wright
8. Ray Williams 9. Roland Malin 10. Brian Ireson 11. Ivan Oakey 12. Cyril Martin 13. Neil Cochrane 14. Jim Davies
15. Eric Thomason 16. Len Davies 17. Frank Foster 18. Frank Fielding 19. Tom Atkins 20. Bert Coward 21. Betty Cochrane
22. Joyce Barnes 23. Grace Oakey 24. Millie Ireson 25. Dora Clarke 26. Eva Warren 27. Sylvia Collins 28. Rene Shears

The Club House and Bowling Green
on the site of the old Vicarage
croquet lawn, 1982

The Club was originally for PSL employees only, but was opened up to non-employees if vacancies arose. Today, the membership consists mainly of Roade residents but some come from further afield.

Short Mat Bowls

Roade Rollers Short Mat Bowls Club was formed in 1994 at Roade School and later moved to the Village Hall. It now has two daytime and two evening County League Teams. One of the night teams, Roade Runners, has recently been promoted to the 1st Division of the South Northants League. The Club is thriving with members aged from 14 to the late 80s who play in competitions all year round and also raise funds for local charities.

Chris Clayson in action at the Village Hall in 2006 (Pat Brittle and Peter Martin in background)

A competition with visiting teams at Roade School, mid 1990s

TENNIS
Roade Tennis Club

Roade Tennis Club was formed early in the 1990s and manages three all-weather courts and a club house in Bailey Brooks Lane which members are able to use throughout the year.

The Club organises annual tournaments and, by membership of the Northampton Tennis League, is able to play at league level. Junior members can receive coaching from a qualified LTA Coach.

The Club is a member of the Lawn Tennis Association, offering opportunities for inter-club competitions and the possibility of entering the ballot for allocations of tickets for the Wimbledon Championships.

Roade Tennis Courts and Club House

FISHING
Pianoforte Supplies Fishing Club

Soon after the end of the Second World War, several keen anglers working at Pianoforte Supplies formed a Fishing Club. The Club, with a membership of 40 plus, proved very popular and competitions and contests were held throughout the season.

Open competitions regularly attracted over 80 contestants.

At first the Club rented water at Showsley, near Towcester, and later a stretch of water on the River Tove, near Castlethorpe. The club no longer exists.

PSL Fishing Club, 1940s

Left to right: Sid Pacey, Sid Watson, unknown, George Simpson, Les Chambers, Len Davies, Ted Ellenburg, unknown, Gilbert Tarry with Derek Tarry sitting at the front

PSL Fishing Club, 1940s

1. Oliver Bowdidge
2. Cyril Cripps
3. Gilbert Tarry
4. Ted Ellenburgh
5. Derek Tarry
6. George Simpson
7. Chapman Gross
8. Len Davies
9. Sid Watson
10. John Wimpress
11. Tess Wilson

Tim Stockdale,
Olympic Show Jumper

For Tim Stockdale, the road to international show-jumping stardom began as an enthusiastic seven year old at Nottinghamshire's Grove Pony Club.

His major breakthrough came when he won the AIT Class at the Royal Windsor Horse Show and, in 1996, won no less than 6 Grand Prix Competitions. Since then Tim has run his thriving yard at Dovecote Farm, assisted by his wife, Laura, and a staff of four.

In 2000, Tim was involved in the Channel 4 series, 'Faking It!' He returned to TV in 2006 for the BBC Sports Relief programme, 'Only Fools on Horses', training celebrities to compete in a televised show jumping competition.

As a member of the British Nations Cup Team, international honours have been regularly won but Tim regards his selection to represent Great Britain, with his horse 'Corlato', at the 2008 Olympic Games in China, as an exceptional career achievement. His sights are now set on competing at the London 2012 Olympics.

Tim Stockdale on Glenwood Springs, 2003

Tim riding 'Corlato' at the 2008 Olympics in China
(photo Trevor Meeks)

CHAPTER 15

Festivities

The earliest recorded village festival commemorated the nativity of St. Mary the Virgin, patron saint of the parish church, and was called Roade Feast. It began on the first Sunday after 19th September and lasted at least a week. *'Stupid buffoonery - donkey races, grinning* (?gurning) *through collars, smoking matches and other disgusting pastimes'* are mentioned as typical activities of Northamptonshire folk at play in the 1830s, and Roade's celebrations are unlikely to have differed. The 'buffoonery' would have been magnified by the presence at that time of over eight hundred navvies employed to dig the railway cutting, camped out in huts in a nearby field.

7 Church End

Later that century the village priest, the Revd. Maze Gregory, set himself to provide more respectable entertainment. During the 1863 Feast Week there were three services on Sunday, with a Monday afternoon harvest thanksgiving service, followed by sports, then evening music, dance and other entertainments at the schoolroom, now No 7 Church End.

On Tuesday there was a flower and vegetable show. On Wednesday, Thursday and Friday evenings the schoolroom was open from seven to ten for music and other entertainments. As a result of the vicar's efforts it was reported that pub takings in Roade had fallen by at least £120 that week.

The parish reading room (probably also at No 7 Church End) put on entertainments all the year round. The 1866 Roade Church Almanack reported that four reading and music entertainments and two exhibitions of Dissolving Views and Magic lantern had been held there the previous

Roade Church Almanack, 1866

Item 105 in 'Odds and Ends', a scrapbook compiled by the Revd. Gregory *(NL 4107, 1-8)*

"Roade" Song, Item 33 in Odds and Ends *(NRO 4107, 1-8)*

winter. The "Roade" song was probably written by the Revd. Gregory, and was performed at a concert given by the Roade Choir on 12th Jan 1863.

Later (according to Job Sturgess) the Feast embraced a two-day Show, the first day being for horticulture, eggs, butter, etc., the second being for sports, etc., which was open to people living within a radius of six miles and included entries from Northampton. The chief organiser was Mr Elden, headmaster of the village school from 1879 to 1922. A less high-minded event was the Feast Monday cricket match between the Tailor's and Baker's teams, with the baker's peel (a long-handled shovel) and the tailor's sleeveboard used as bats. Villagers would join in the fielding, much beer was drunk, and no result was ever achieved. Afterwards there was dancing in the Swan Field, the local quoits ground, presumably on land by the Swan pub, and few went to bed before midnight.

Another feature of Feast week was Sheppard's Fair in the Railway field, part of the land later occupied by Walkerpack, with a little pony to work the roundabouts. Its venue then became the recreation field, with continued annual visits until the late 1970s.

The Revd. Gregory also instituted a village holiday in the summer, which began after a special service with a 'monster tea party' in the vicarage grounds. In 1864 nearly 600 sat down to tea and over 1,000 were present. Activities included cricket, sports, games and dancing till dark. One of the most popular events was the flat race for old women, with prizes of up to half a pound of tea. Many local clergy and gentry participated in the sports and games. In 1863 H. Wake won a pocket knife in the boys' sack race.

St Mary's Church Fete, now Thanksgiving, still takes place in the summer but at a much lower key than the village holiday. A Community Fete is also now held at the Ex-Servicemen's Club near the beginning of July.

Nora Gray, sack race

Not always pulling together

All little boys wanted to be an engine driver (Brian Reeve with engine he built)

Mrs Tipler (left) and Mrs Robinson at the Soft Toys Stall

The whole village joined in patriotic celebrations, such as Queen Victoria's Diamond Jubilee, and other national festivals.

Above: Celebrating Queen Victoria's Diamond Jubilee, High Street, 1897

Right: Empire Day, 1909

Local children addressed by Sir Herewald Craufurd Wake, Bart. Empire Day was celebrated on Queen Victoria's birthday, 24th May, although it was not instituted until after her death

Boys at Pageant, 1937

Parade celebrating the Coronation of King George VI and Queen Elizabeth, 1937

The Cock, Coronation Day, 1953

The Coronations in 1937 and 1953 were celebrated in the old vicarage grounds with sports, games and a pageant, as well as the obligatory refreshment of tea.

At the end of European hostilities in 1945, on VE Day, Tommy Lane entertained customers at the George with his accomplished gurning, demonstrating the persistence of Roade's ancient way of celebration!

ROADE VILLAGE
Coronation Festivities Committee.
QUEEN ELIZABETH II. JUNE 2ND, 1953.
Chairman : C. T. Cripps M.B.E.

PROGRAMME:

9-45 a.m. to 10-15 a.m.	COMBINED MORNING SERVICE. Conducted by The Rev. N. Husbands, supported by The Methodist & Baptist Churches.
1-30 p.m. to 3-30 p.m.	CHILDRENS' SPORTS. Prizes to the value of £15 Organised by Mr. R. Harper.
3-30 p.m. to 5-30 p.m.	ADULTS' GAMES & SPORTS. Prizes to the value of £18.—Special Attraction for Tug of War Teams. Prizes value £5. Organised by The Cricket & Youth Clubs.
4-15 p.m. to 5-15 p.m.	CHILDRENS' TEA & PRESENTATION OF SOUVENIRS. Organised by The Mothers Union.
5 p.m. to 6 p.m.	HIGH TEA FOR "DARBYS & JOANS". Organised by Mrs. K. M. Gross & Helpers.
6-30 p.m. to 8 p.m.	PAGEANT. "ELIZABETH I — ELIZABETH II" Presented by Roade Women's Institute & Roade Amateur Dramatic Society.
8-15 p.m.	WHIST DRIVE. — GOOD PRIZES. (Refreshments Provided.) Organised by The British Legion. (Womens' Section.)
9 p.m. to 1 a.m.	DANCE. (Refreshments Provided.) Organised by Messrs. C. H. & C. J. Webb.
10-30 p.m.	BONFIRE & FIREWORKS. Organised by The British Legion. (Mens Section).

The Sports, Games and Pageant will be held in the Vicarage Grounds, and a Refreshment Marquee will be available in the afternoon for Beer, Minerals, Tea & Coffee. Ice Cream will be provided for the Children.

In the event of inclement weather an alternative Programme for the Childrens' Sports will be arranged.

The Expenses of the whole Programme will be borne from Funds raised by the Committee.

The Music for the Sports, Games & Pageant etc., also the amplifying equipment is being provided by the courtesy of Mr. R. Munns.

Programme for 1953 Coronation festivities

Turner's Butcher's Shop decked out for the 1953 Coronation

Baptist Bus outing, 1948

There were also celebrations at various venues, including the Village Hall, for the Silver Jubilee in 1977.

The site of the former vicarage is now occupied by the Bowling Club which hosts many parties, hog-roasts and similar events.

Baptist fete, 1965

The Baptists, too, held bazaars, fetes, outings and parties as fund-raisers and for fun. The Band of Hope mounted entertainments in the chapel, such as Munn's Magic Lantern. Memorable Annual Sunday School Treats included a trip to Blisworth, presumably to the pleasure gardens, when the railway opened, and another to Bugbrooke in 1914 for a Wireless and Telegraphy exhibition. There were great celebrations with numerous visiting preachers on the 200th and 250th anniversaries of the chapel's foundation in 1688.

Baptists with loaves in Stone House garden

Boy's Brigade group

The Methodists also had numerous functions to fund construction of their chapel and pay for its furnishings, two organs, and refurbishment. They held many entertainments - Sunday School and Boy's Brigade outings, dramas, fetes and recitals. Until recently, Stainer's 'Crucifixion' and 'The Road to Calvary' were sung in alternate years.

S. Humphrey, Methodist Dickensian fete, 1980

Methodist Christmas, 1957

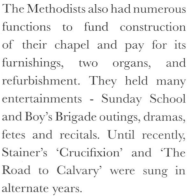

Methodist drama, 1967

Primary School Fete

The village school held open days, fetes, vegetable shows and carnivals in which pupils and staff participated. It won the Gardening Shield in competitions many times in the 1930s, and in the 1940s, Music Certificates from County Singing Festivals.

Aerial View of the Village Institute centre behind Warwick House, 1974

The Village Institute, founded in 1885 on land donated by the Grafton Estate, hosted many whist drives, magic lantern shows and dances until its closure in the 1970s. St Mary's Church Hall and the Village Hall in Bailey Brooks Lane continue to host numerous social and educational events.

The British Legion met in a wooden hut near St Mary's Church. It had previously been used at Courteenhall School during World War II and was moved to Roade when no longer required. The move to the current site in Bailey Brooks Lane was the result of the Wake family providing land for a new Club House. Numerous functions, music, dance and theatre, are still held there.

PSL Children's Party Invitation, 1949

PSL Canteen group, 1950

The factory canteen, opened in 1938, became a centre for staff and their families' entertainment with its sprung maple floor and billiards room, and was also used as a lecture-room, theatre, dance, social hall and dining room. Many whist drives and entertainments were mounted there.

Cripps House, in The Ridings, was opened in the late 1960s and hosts events for residents of the nearby sheltered bungalows, Roade Evergreens, and for many others, such as the W.I., the Wine Club, and the Painting Group.

Cripps House, 2009

Weddings have long been a time for joy and celebration and so it has been for the villagers of Roade.

CHAPTER 16

Weddings

The essence of marriage has not changed over the centuries, namely the exchange of promises between a man and a woman in front of witnesses.

Until the Reformation, the State had no direct involvement. In 1538 each Parish was ordered to keep Registers of Baptisms, Weddings and Funerals and the State became increasingly involved, although until 1753 it was still possible for a marriage to be by affirmation before witnesses. Legal proof of such marriages could be difficult.

From 1753 until 1837 a marriage had to take place in an Anglican (Established) church to be legally recognised except for Quaker or Jewish marriages. In 1837 civil registration was introduced and marriages could be solemnised in a church other than that of the Church of England, provided that a Civil Registrar was present. This continued until the middle of the twentieth century when representatives of other denominations could be registered to preside at weddings. Weddings can now be held in places other than churches, provided they are registered for the purpose.

Weddings have long been a time for joy and celebration and so it has been for the villagers of Roade. Here are a few pictures of the weddings of local people in various churches in and around Roade.

Robert Cozens and Winifred Mackie - *1923*

Robert Cozens lived at Burman Farm. Winifred Mackie was his second wife.

Sid Parish and Florence Nightingale - *1925*

Sid was the youngest of 8 children and was born in a cottage in White Hart Yard in 1897. The row of cottages, which adjoined the former White Hart Public House (now Roade House Restaurant and Hotel), has since been demolished. He drove a horse-drawn ambulance in the First World War and after the war came back to Roade and lived with his mother in the same cottage. He was the only child still living at home when his mother died. Florence was born in Weedon and came to Roade when she was ten. Sid died at home in 1960 having lived his whole life, with the exclusion of his war service, in the cottage where he was born. They were married in the Baptist Chapel at Roade.

Left to right: Groom's brother Joe Goodridge (Best Man), Linda Bird (friend of the bride), Groom and Bride, Bride's brother, Stan Lenton, who gave her away, and Bridesmaid (unknown) and friend of the bride

Ernest John (Jack) Goodridge and Gladys Lenton - *August 1929*

This photograph was taken in front of the bride's home at Memorial Green. Gladys was not born in Roade, but moved to the village from Northampton. Jack came from Shutlanger and after the wedding they lived with Gladys's mother in the cottage in the photo.

They were married in St Mary's Church, Roade, and the service was conducted by the Revd William Sharland.

Ernie Kedwards and Annie Elizabeth Skears

The wedding took place c1930. The bridesmaid second from the left is Millie Henman and Reg Skears, the bride's brother, is on the far right. The couple lived in Ivor Terrace in the High Street.

Bob Heighway and Dorothy (Dolly) Poole - *August 1940*

Left to right: The boy sitting on the gate is Teddy Lewis. He and his brother were evacuees and lived with Dolly's family for 6 years until the end of the war

Cyril Johnson - Best Man and married to Dolly's sister, Bridesmaid - bride's niece, Groom and Bride, Harry Poole - brother of the bride who gave her away, Bridesmaid - bride's niece

The Wedding photograph was taken in The Leys

The wedding was during the war. It was fortunate for Dolly that clothes rationing did not start until 1941. Many war-time brides had great difficulty acquiring sufficient clothing coupons needed when buying a wedding dress. Dolly also remembers that after the cake had been made it had to be carried back to the house in a tin bath. They were married at St Mary's Church, Roade.

Frank Ablett and Nancy Barnes - *27th June 1942*

Nancy came from Roade, Frank from Ipswich and they met through Nancy's brother-in-law, Ray Warren. Even though the wedding took place during World War II, Nancy cannot recall any difficulty obtaining her wedding dress or those for the bridesmaids. She said that she "just went to town and bought them". Frank was based in England at the time of the wedding but he had to leave Roade at 4am on the day after their wedding to get back to his Unit. They were married in St Mary's Church at Roade. Canon Husbands officiated.

Left to right: Bridesmaid Evelyn Etheridge who came from Ipswich, Best Man - Eric Humphries, Groom and Bride, Bride's father - Ernest Thomas Barnes, Bridesmaid Eva - Bride's sister

Gordon Battams and Ruby Wilson - 18th March 1950

Ruby Wilson's Red Cross colleagues formed a Guard of Honour.

Left to right: Jean Cozens, Mrs Anderson, Emily Shipman (Skears), Bette Shipman, Mrs Maxwell, Isabel Watford, Gladys Goodridge and Edna Cozens

Left to right: Mrs Nightingale- Groom's maternal grandmother, John Denny- Best Man, Mrs Florence Parish- Groom's mother, Bridesmaid- Bride's cousin, Ray and Sylvia- Bride and Groom, Mrs Sarah Bodaly- Bride's mother, Joy Hartnell- Bridesmaid, Richard Lane- Bride's brother in law, Frederick Bodaly- Bride's father, Margaret Lane- Bride's sister.

(N.B. Photo ❶ is Ray's parents' wedding)

Ray Parish and Sylvia Bodaly - 8th April 1950

Ray was born in Roade and Sylvia lived in Wootton. They were married in her home village at St Georges Church and after their marriage set up home together in Roade.

Bill Piper and Dorothy Mason - *30th December 1950*

Bill was born in London and, at age 12, was evacuated to Roade during World War II. When the evacuees arrived at Pianoforte Supplies' canteen, none of the waiting 'foster mothers' picked Bill and it was dark by the time he was taken round the village.

He was taken to Mrs Parish's cottage in White Hart Lane and, without hesitation, she said that she would take him. Dorothy was born in Ashton but came to Roade while she was a toddler. Her father had a cobbler's shop in South View opposite the Cock Public House. Bill decided very early on that he would stay in Roade and he did not return to London after the war. His first job was in his future father-in-law's cobbler's shop.

Bill and Dorothy were married at St Mary's Church, Roade.

Left to right:
Mrs Florence Parish,
Bridesmaid, Best Man -
Ray Parish, Groom and Bride,
Bridesmaid, Bridesmaid,
Bride's mother and father
- Mrs and Mr Mason

Left to right: Groom's mother
and father - Ethel and John
Gardner, Groom's sister -
Eveline (Eva), Best Man, Groom
and Bride, Bride's father -
Cyril Thomas Cripps (later Sir
Cyril Cripps), Bride's sister
- Joan, Bride's mother -
Amy (later Lady Cripps)

Lesley John (Jack) Gardner and Elizabeth (Betty) Mary Cripps - *9th June 1951*

The bride and groom's families lived in the village and the couple continued to live in Roade after their wedding. The bride's father was the founder of Pianoforte Supplies Limited. The groom's mother and sister ran a general store from the front room of their cottage in Yew Tree Terrace. Sadly the groom died aged only 27 in August 1953.

Left to right: Tom Oakey – the bride's brother-in-law holding his daughter Thelma, names of next 4 people are unknown, Groom, Bride's sister Hilda (Mrs Tom Oakey), Bride, names of next two people are unknown, Bride's parents - Mr and Mrs Leach

Alfred Day and Edna Leach - *married in 1951 or 1952*

Edna was born in Roade and Alf came from Kent. He served in the army in World War II and at some time after demobilisation settled in the Hardingstone area. After their marriage, they lived in Roade. They were the first residents of 29 Hyde Close, which was one of the council houses built in the expansion of Roade after the war, and they lived there for their entire married life. They were married at St Edmund's Church, Hardingstone.

Cecil Patrick and Margaret Lane - *19th May 1956*

Margaret and her father, Arthur, are shown arriving at St Mary's Church, Roade. They are on the footpath in Church End leading to the church gate. Churchcroft had not yet been developed as a housing estate and so the current church car park did not exist. Margaret was born in Wrights Yard (then off High Street, between No 37 and No 43). Several generations of her family, back to her maternal and paternal great grandparents, were born in Roade. Cecil came from Collingtree and the couple set up home in Roade.

Richard Johnson and Margaret Goodridge - *28th March 1959*

Margaret was born and grew up in Roade. Richard's family moved from London to Roade during the Second World War.

Left to right - Back row: Groom's parents - Mr and Mrs Johnson, Best Man - Eddie Dennis, Groom and Bride, Bride's parents - Mr and Mrs Goodridge

Front row: Bridesmaids Anne and Astrid Smekens, a family friend and Linda Johnson (Groom's niece)

(N.B. Photo ❷ is Margaret's parents' wedding)

Left to right: John Fitchett holding his daughter Anne, his wife Sheila, Groom's parents – Ted and Marjorie Curtis, Bride's sister – Wendy, Best Man – Mike Connolly, Bride's sister – Suzanne, Groom and Bride, Bride's cousins – Shirley Geeson and Rene Phipps, Bride's brothers – David and Peter, Bride's parents – George and Edith Phipps

Donald Curtis and Yvonne Phipps - *12th March 1960*

Don was born in London where his father Ted worked as a goods guard on the railway; although both his parents had lived in Roade as children. His mother moved back to Roade early in World War II and Ted followed when their house was flattened in the blitz. Don's grandfather, William Henry Sharland, was Vicar of Roade from 1908 to 1936. Yvonne was born in Northampton and the couple were married at St Mary's Church, Dallington Village, Northampton. They spent the first 47 years of their married life in Roade until they moved to a bungalow in Northampton in 2007.

Bill Hudson and Jean Collins - *3rd June 1961*

Jean was born in Roade and Bill moved to the village when his father became the Manager of Roade Co-op in Hartwell Road. They were married in St Mary's Church, Roade. Canon Husbands officiated.

John Collins and Ruth Lyon - *18th May 1963*

This was the first wedding in Roade Methodist Chapel following a change in the law. Previously a Registrar was required to be present when the ceremony took place in a church or chapel other than of the Established Church (Church of England).

John was born in Roade and Ruth came from Northampton. They met through the Methodist Church.

Left to right: Ray Holdsworth - Best Man, Groom and Bride, Shirley Reeve and Ann Molcher

**Dave Merchant and Theresa Ablett -
3rd September 1966**

Theresa and Dave first met at Roade Primary School when he moved from Northampton. Theresa was born in the village.

Canon Norman Husbands officiated at the Wedding in St Mary's Church, Roade and is shown handing the couple their Wedding Certificate.

Three smart young guests at Dave and Theresa's Wedding
Left to right: Bride's cousins Trevor Warren and Colin Barnes and Bride's brother Malcolm Ablett

(N.B. Photo ❸ is Theresa's parents' wedding)

**Alvin Barby and
Brenda Sturgess -
11th October 1975**

Brenda was born in Roade and Alvin moved into the village from Courteenhall in 1962. They started married life at "Cornerstones" next to the Methodist Church. The house was an office for Roddis Steam Engine and Agricultural Equipment before being converted in 1930 into a residence.

Left to right: In front - the three bridesmaids (bride's nieces) were Helen Gent, Emma Gent and Susan Sturgess. Best Man David Lee, Groom's parents Lucy and Frank Barby, Groom and Bride, Bride's parents Emily and John Sturgess.

Left to right- mainly serving Royal Engineers (exceptions marked)

Ben Dillon, Craig Appleby,Geoff Ward MBE (retired Lt Col), Mike Thorn (Royal Marine), Glyn Hannah, ,Groom and Bride, Stuart (Chalky) White, Dave Thorne (Best Man and Royal Marine) Neil Melloy, Baz Lapthorne, Dave Malyan, Scottie Clelland, Nigel (super Nige) Martin, Lance Butress.

Paul Ward and Andrea Mawby - *26th May 2001*

Andrea, the daughter of Peter and Sylvia Mawby, was born in Northampton but grew up in Roade. Paul was born in Bournemouth and he grew up in Hemel Hempstead. They were married in St Mary's Church, Roade. Andrea met Paul through mutual friends after she left university to work at Bart's Hospital, London

Sadly, Craig Appleby, one of the Guard of Honour, died on 11th November 2007 while working in the Lebanon carrying out civilian humanitarian de-mining.

CHAPTER 17

Roade at War

Two of the most visible legacies of the World Wars are a Memorial on the Green where the Ashton and Hartwell Roads fork, and the Ex-Servicemen's Club in Bailey Brooks Lane.

Unveiling Service

The Memorial and Green are maintained by the Parish Council, the flower beds at various times by Roade Branch of the British Legion, Roade Scouts and currently by Roade Allotments Association.

Before the Second World War, a full service with pedal organ accompaniment was held on the Green each Armistice Day.

Unveiling the memorial, 1921

Unveiling ceremony

Memorial Green

Eight Roade casualties of World War I and eight of World War II are named on the monument (unveiled 1921). Another ten who died in World War I and one in World War II have since been identified, and are included in the Roade Roll of Honour produced by Gordon Hall and the Local History Society in 2008.

Roade Royal British Legion Branch was so popular that men enrolled while still in the forces. At first it met in the Swan pub, beside the railway, then moved to a hut off Church End in 1946.

British Legion hut,
(lower right corner of photograph)

In 1969 it moved to its present location in Bailey Brooks Lane, operating as The Ex-Servicemen's Club as well as HQ of the Branch. In 2009 there were over 400 Club and 150 Branch members.

Leaning on the church wall by the hut

British Legion – opening day

During World War 1 almost 100 Roade men are known to have served in the forces.

Many would have been volunteers, such as Sid Parish, who gave his age as 18 when he was only 16. Others joined the Northampton Citizen Corps, which was affiliated to the Central Association Volunteer Training Corps (the equivalent of the World War II Home Guard). In January 1916 the Military Service Act imposed conscription on single men aged 18 to 41, except for religious ministers, conscientious objectors and those medically unfit or in essential war time employment. Job Sturgess, then a farm manager, shepherd and milk retailer, was exempt because he was *employed in a certified occupation*. He was an early member of the Citizen Corps and from 1916 to 1919 was a Private in the volunteer section of the 1st Battalion, Northamptonshire Regiment.

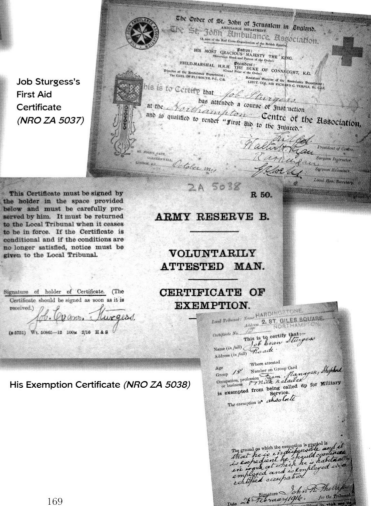

Job Sturgess's First Aid Certificate (NRO ZA 5037)

His Exemption Certificate (NRO ZA 5038)

Roade men who served in World War I – list at back of Parish Council Minute Book (NRO 281P/502)

Jesse Higgins, 1916

Sid Parish

Bill Humphrey, 1915

Ray Parish

Ron Tomkins, R.M.

Richard (Dick) Dyke, 1944

Bill Botwood, 1940

Just over twenty years later Roade men served in front-line action or support in most theatres of World War II and occupied territories. For example, Dick Dyke participated in the audacious and successful D-Day glider landings to take and hold Pegasus Bridge, and after active service in Burma, Ray Parish was stationed at Kure, near Hiroshima, in 1946.

Stan Tapp in India, 1943

There were two recorded military incidents at Roade during World War II.

A stick of four bombs fell between the railway and Hyde Farm, shattering the glazing of the newly-built council houses along Grafton Road. It was rumoured that the bomber was shot down near Weedon.

A Wellington with six-man Canadian crew was struck by lightning in 1944 and came down by the 'Scratter', near Ashton Road, killing all aboard.

Don & Bob Gray

INVASION!

A PUBLIC MEETING

WILL BE HELD ON

SUNDAY EVENING, JULY 19th,

1942, at 8 o'clock prompt,

In the Council Schools, Roade, when the Village Invasion Committee will report on the steps taken, or to be taken, for your protection in the event of Blitz or Invasion.

Sir Hereward Wake, Bart.

has kindly consented to attend and speak.

Every Adult Parishioner is invited and urged to be present.

Invasion fears
persisted well
after 1940

The Home Guard and Auxiliary Fire Service had sections in Roade, based in the vicarage and its stables, and the former carried out training exercises every Sunday morning. One mock attack near the Post Office involved tanks, thunderflashes and smoke bombs.

Home Guard

Burned out station

The AFS assisted with local fires. Once, returning from an exercise in London, as their train pulled in at Roade station, they found the booking office had caught fire in their absence and was gutted.

Fortunately neither body saw enemy action, though Roade cutting was included as a strategic target in the cancelled Nazi invasion plan, Operation Sealion.

Carrying on!

The German illustration and description of Roade Railway Cutting was included in 'the important and vulnerable points' in Britain pictured and described in a Top Secret 'Guide Book' to Britain prepared by the German Military for the use of their invading and occupation forces.

GB8, B23, No 55. 'The Railway Cutting near Blisworth (Northamptonshire) The 2.5km long Cutting with several lines of the London Midland & Scottish Railway, between Blisworth and Roade, South from Northampton, is 19.8metres deep. In the background is an old flat, arched road bridge.

The Luftwaffe do not seem to have taken the trouble to reconnoitre the target, but merely copied a contemporary picture of the Cutting as it was when first opened, complete with ancient steam locomotive!

PSL children's party, 1948

The World Wars had profound effects on daily life in Roade. Rationing of food and clothes impinged directly on residents, as did the Dig for Victory campaign.

Children's party, 1946

Gladys Goodridge 1943

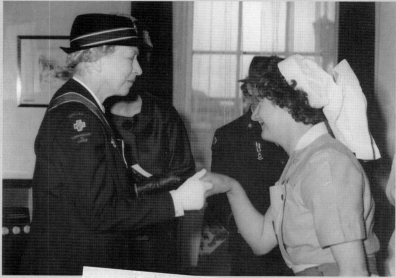

Dolly Savage &
Princess Royal

The factory canteen and Church Institute on High Street ran frequent whist drives and other fund-raising events for war charities. Ancillary arms - Air Raid Wardens, the Red Cross (which had a large detachment

WI Recipe

WOMEN'S LAND ARMY (ENGLAND & WALES).
RELEASE CERTIFICATE.
The Women's Land Army for England and Wales acknowledges
with appreciation the services given by

Miss Hilda Leach

who has been an enrolled member for the period from

21st May 1947 to 15th May 1948

and has this day been granted a willing release.

Date 15th May 1948

WOMEN'S LAND ARMY

```
                    W A R T I M E
        During the war years the village received many evacuees,
mainly from London.  Many of them joined the W.I. and were very
active members, especially with the Drama Section and organising
pageants.  Some meetings were held in the old British Legion
wooden hut alongside the church footpath, and others in the Baptist
Church Rooms or in the Primary School
                    ***************

        Food shortages and rationing brought many difficulties for
housewives and the W.I. devised many new recipes. Here is a wartime
recipe for one of our Competitions:-
            Chocolate Sponge Cake - NO EGGS

Ingredients: 1½ Cupfuls S.R. flour
             1   Tablespoon Sugar
             2      "     Golden Syrup
             2   Dessertspoons Cocoa         Bake for 20 minutes.
             1      "       Vinegar
             ¼ teaspoon Bi-carbonate of Soda
             1 cup of Milk
             Filling:
             1 Tablespoon Sugar
             1    "     Cocoa
             1 Nut of margarine
             1 Dessertspoon Hot Water.
                    ***************

        Roade W.I. had a very good choir during the war years which
sang in the schools, at the Y.W.C.A. in Northampton, and also visited
other villages.  The Conductor was Mrs. O. Coward and the Leader
was Mrs. Blamire.
        The Drama Group produced many plays during this period, among
the most successful of which was "Gypsies"

        Mrs. E. Scotts, of 14 London Road, was in charge of the canning
machine and members would go along to her house to can surplus fruit
and vegetables.  Some of our members were still using this machine
for the same purposes even into the 1960's.
                    *****************

        Mrs.R.Walker, a founder member, recalls that before the war
refreshments were usually a cup of tea, sandwiches and cakes, but
war-time rationing stopped all that, and even printed programmes had
to be discontinued.
        Our Institute had a thriving Produce Guild, of which Mrs. R.
Walker was secretary, and they supported the W.I.Market in Northampton.
In common with many other organisations, Roade W.I. organised a very
successful National Savings Group.
        Not all was gloom during the war years for we had many happy
outings by train, for example a much enjoyed visit to Lady Wernher's
house at Luton Hoo, and a number of plays and pageants were produced.
Rehearsals for these were usually held in the Baptist Church Rooms,
and the Pageants paraded through the village.
```

Nora Gray

of women in Roade helping in hospitals, transport and fund-raising) the W.V.S., and Women's Land Army, all demanded extra time and/or changes of work from villagers. Many were posted away from Roade.

PSL in 1950

The PSL factory began war production in 1937, and by 1940 was almost entirely devoted to production of military pyrotechnics and parts. C.T. Cripps was awarded the M.B.E. for his company's contribution to the war effort. The RAF Unit in Salcey Forest also employed locals for maintenance and repair work before call-up. The Foreign Office Communications Centre at Hanslope employed locals, and still does today. The top-secret code-cracking unit at Bletchley Park may also have drawn on Roade for personnel, though no information is available.

An enduring result of wartime upheavals was the settlement in Roade of at least nine evacuee families and several ex-POWs, who married and raised families here. One evacuee, Jim Howard, ran the village newsagents, and for several years was Chairman of the Parish Council and the Old Folks Fund.

Jim Howard

The evacuees arrived in two waves, the first immediately after declaration of war in 1939, when a hundred children arrived, only for most to return home during the phoney war, the second fleeing the London and Coventry blitzes. At first there were too many pupils for normal primary classes, so the school day was split, locals in the morning, evacuees in the afternoon. Even so, others had to be accommodated in the Church Institute and Methodist and Baptist rooms, with the very youngest in a back room at the George. Gradually numbers fell, and school returned to a more normal routine with added staff, and at least one, Mrs Malin, from the evacuees' old school. Some children, on reaching the school-leaving age of 14, took jobs at PSL rather than return home.

At the end of European hostilities in 1945, Tommy Lane entertained customers in the George with his accomplished 'gurning' - a testimony to the persistence of Roade's age-old customary celebrations!

Evacuees Jean and Pat Coker being visited by their mother, 1942

Vic Johnson, evacuee

Rationing lingered on long after World War II, and only with a new decade, perhaps marked by the Festival of Britain in 1951 and the Coronation in 1953, did wartime attitudes begin to fade, superseded by fresh preoccupations, housing, work, courtship, family, politics, Rock 'n' Roll, the Cold War and the threat of nuclear war. But, like the rest of the world, Roade and its inhabitants were changed irrevocably by the events of both World Wars.

Roade Local History Society has published *Roade Roll of Honour* commemorating 27 of our men who died in the two World Wars. Copies are kept in St Mary's and Roade Methodist Churches.

CHAPTER 18

Farms

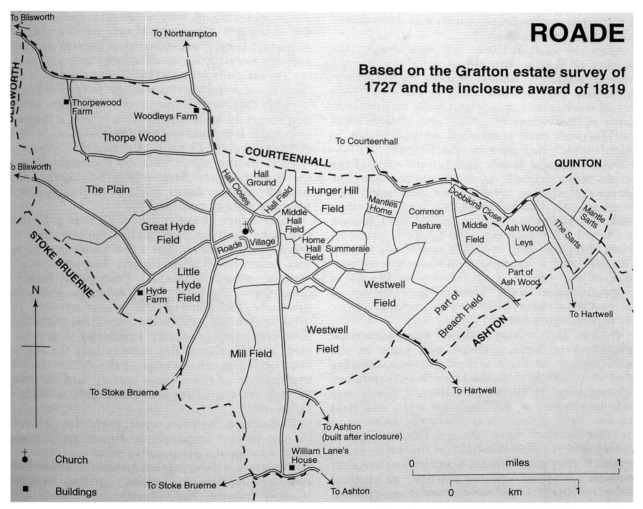

Map showing open fields in Roade reproduced from A History of the County of Northampton Vol. Five. (Boydell & Brewer Ltd, 2002), p.347, by permission of the Executive Editor

Open Fields

In medieval times there appear to have been two open field systems in the parish, one belonging to Hyde manor and another shared by other estates with land around the village. By the 18th century the two systems had been combined and the farming of the common fields was regulated by the Grafton Manor Court (although only about half belonged to the Grafton Estate). In addition to the common fields there were some 'old inclosures', mainly in areas of former woodland in the north-west and north- east of the parish. Traces of 'ridge-and-furrow' survive in some parts of the parish, including the Recreation Field.

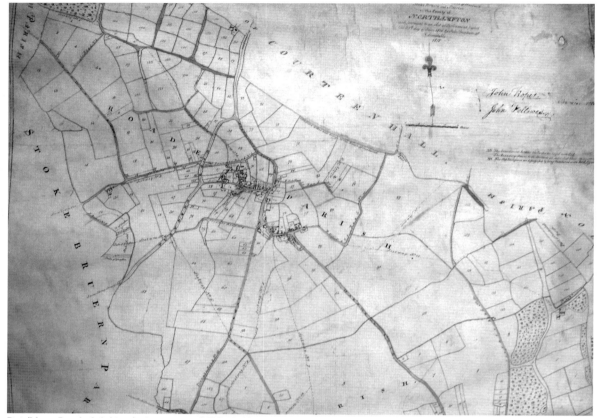

Detail from Roade & Ashton inclosure map *(NRO 4218)*

Inclosure of the Open Fields

By the end of the 18th century, agriculture in Roade was described as being *'in a wretched state, from the land being in common fields: the farmers are often at a great loss for hay; their cows, in the summer, must be herded on the head-lands in the daytime and confined in the night; their crops of corn are scanty; and their land by constant tillage becomes almost exhausted. In short they are of opinion that were their lands enclosed and their rents doubled they should be considerable gainers.'*
Sir Frederic Eden writing about Roade in "The State of the Poor", published in 1797.

The open fields of Roade and Ashton were inclosed between 1816 and 1819. At that time the Grafton Estate owned about 520 acres of land in Roade, mainly in the east of the parish, and about 35 houses and cottages in the village. Other major landholders included Robert Cave (farmer); the vicars of Roade, Hartwell and Ashton; Worcester College, Oxford (which owned Thorpewood Farm); Elizabeth Paggett (heiress of The Cock); Stephen Warwick (farmer and owner of Hyde Farm); Stephen Blunt (farmer) and Sir William Wake. Ten others owned between 10 and 55 acres, including the Corporation of Northampton and the two local charities. Altogether 26 owners received allotments of land in the former open

fields while others, such as John Markham, owner of the New Inn (later Woodleys), held only land which had already been inclosed. There is no record of objections to the inclosure of Roade, although there may have been some. In 1817, 1 rood and 9 perches were deducted from land being sold by the Duke of Grafton to Sir William Wake in order to provide gardens for some of the Duke's cottages *'much required, in consequence of some of their former gardens having been took away, from being open field property'*.

No new farmhouses were built in the parish as a result of inclosure and during the 19th century the Grafton farms there were gradually consolidated into Burman Farm.

Hyde Farm House, Hyde Road

Hyde Farm House dates from the 14th century, when it had a solar (parlour), hall, cross passage, service bay and porch. The manor of Hyde then belonged to the Augustinian abbey of St James in Duston, which had owned land in and around Hyde and Roade since the middle of the twelfth century. The abbey also owned two thirds of Roade church and the whole of the chapel at Hartwell. The Hyde manor would have provided food for the abbey - the remains of fishponds can still be seen south west of the house.

After the abbey was dissolved the manor was owned by the Fermors of Easton Neston and then by the Hoes and their Warwick and Henshaw descendants. By the end of the 18th century, the house and most of the land had passed to Stephen Warwick, whose father had inherited Hyde from the Revd

Hyde Farm House, c.1862

Stephen Hoe Henshaw on condition that he have his son baptised and brought up in the Church of England. Stephen Warwick was a substantial farmer who became a prominent Baptist (like other members of his family) and later lived in Warwick House (2 Church End).

Hyde Farm House, c.1920

Members of Roade Baptist church were baptised in the stream at Hyde Farm for many generations.

The house was altered in the 17th century, when an almost detached two-storey dairy (now the kitchen) was added at the north-east corner, the porch was remodelled and a chimney stack was inserted in the hall backing onto the cross passage. A cellar was also inserted under the solar at the west end. The old legend that there was a secret underground passage between the manors at Hyde and Ashton has never been substantiated.

Hyde Farm House early 20th century (17th century extension left of porch)

Pond south west of Hyde Farm House

179

Dovecote – early photograph

Hyde Dovecote

South east of the manor is a ruined dovecote. This may be the 'dovehouse' which existed in the early 16th century or a later replacement. Originally it was about 13ft. high with a conical thatched roof. By 1910 the roof of the dovecote had fallen in, although there were still about 380 pigeonholes and the remains of the rotating central post with radiating arms used to reach the nests.

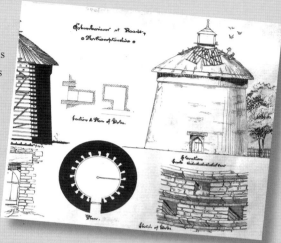

Drawings of Hyde dovecote, 1872
(NRO Ref. P6621)

Benjamin Dunkley and his family lived at the old Hyde Farm in the first half of the 20th century. They were followed by the Thompsons, Yorks and another Dunkley family (not thought to be related to the Ben Dunkleys). In 1972 Peter and Mary Dunkley moved to a new Hyde Farm on Blisworth Road and sold the old Hyde Farm House together with about 25 acres which have since been divided between the old house and Dovecote Farm.

Hyde Farm House and dovecote early 20th century

Mrs Marian Dunkley and friend, c.1920

180

Hyde Farm House (foreground) and Dovecote Farm

Tim Stockdale on Parcival-Jerez, 2002

Dovecote Farm, Hyde Road

Dovecote Farm was built on land formerly belonging to the old Hyde Farm House and is now the home and yard of the international show jumper Tim Stockdale.

Hyde Farm

Hyde Farm, Blisworth Road

Stuart Dunkley took over Hyde Farm from his father, Peter, in 1994 and breeds and fattens pedigree sheep and rare British Dexter and White Park beef cattle. White Park is the oldest beef breed in the country and is connected with the sirloin legend - both Henry VIII and James 1 are said to have 'knighted' a 'surloin' of beef, calling it Sir Loin. Stuart is now the only resident farmer in Roade.

Opposite the farm house, on the other side of Blisworth Road, there is a conservation area of 40 acres of wild flower meadow, which is open to the public. People using the site are asked to follow the Country Code.

Wild flower meadow

Burman Farm, Bretts Lane

Burman Farm once belonged to the Grafton Estate and takes its name from one of the tenants, Thomas Burman, whose debts forced him to quit in 1892. The farm was owned by the Cozens family from 1920 to 1955 and then became the nucleus of the Cripps farming business, which incorporates the land of various farms in Roade, Ashton and Stoke Bruerne. The old Burman farmhouse was sold for residential use in the 1990s.

Burman Farm

Robert Cozens at Burman Farm, late 1940s (his son Bob can be seen in the doorway)

George Cozens and Alan Williams with Bob Cozens on top of the load

Bob Cozens, George Cozens and Bert Watford

L-R George Cozens, Alan Williams, Bob Cozens and Jack Skears

Robert Cozens built up a TT-attested dairy herd of about 60 cows in spite of an early setback when all his cattle, sheep and pigs had to be slaughtered because of foot and mouth. He also bought milk from other farms and delivered to Roade, Ashton, Hartwell, Stoke Bruerne and Shutlanger. At first deliveries were made by tricycle and cart, then by vans until finally the milk was sold to a firm in the town and collected from the farm every morning.

Children were always eager to work and play at Burman Farm.

Children playing in the pond at Burman Farm, early 20th century

Bill Cozens with Arthur Ford at the wheel of a Ferguson tractor and Bill Ford behind

Milk delivery tricycle, identity of children is not known

George Cozens, aged 8, and Captain, 1935

Building a hayrick at Laurel Farm in 1910

Farm carts at Laurel Farm in 1929

Laurel Farm, Hartwell Road

In the 1920s and 30s, William Higgins and his son, Jesse, (Derek Humphrey's grandfather and uncle), managed Laurel Farm in Hartwell Road. It was owned by Mr J O Adams, and a Dr Mason lived in the farmhouse. William and Elizabeth Higgins lived opposite in Pear Tree House. Albert King Cooper was the tenant farmer in 1936 and he stayed for 33 years. He was born in Banbury and had been farming with his father in Shutlanger. When his father died, he wanted a smaller place and came to Roade where he and his son, Gordon, took on the tenancy of Laurel Farm. The farm was later acquired by C T Cripps and added to his existing agricultural property. Burman Farm in Bretts Lane, managed by

Syd and Derek Humphrey "helping out" in 1934

Left to right: Bill Kightley, Jesse Higgins, William Higgins (Farm Manager) with Derek Humphrey & Syd Humphrey in front – Bill, Derek & Syd are grandsons of William

Ben Middleton, gradually expanded to take in hand all the agricultural land associated with Mr Cripps, including Laurel Farm which became the farm manager's residence. By 2005 all the agricultural land had reverted to being leased out.

Horses at Laurel Farm in 1930

William Higgins in his role as bee keeper in 1930 (Stone House in the background)

Elm Farm, High Street

Bert Dunkley bought Elm Farm, situated in the High Street, in 1928. He had previously farmed Hyde Farm with other members of his family. He kept cows pastured in fields along Hyde Road and Blisworth Road. One of these fields was later acquired by Roade Football Club. These fields were part of Elm Farm and Mr Dunkley bought a neighbouring small farm from Mr Sturgess. Bert's son Brian remembers one of his jobs as a young lad of nine or so was to drive the cows down from the fields to Elm Farm for milking. The cattle were taken to a paddock where the telephone exchange now stands, but when he acquired the Sturgess farm it included a cow barn and a Dutch barn. The farm buildings fronting the High Street were demolished in the 1960s when the road was widened. Whilst the farm was still functioning, milk was put into churns and collected daily. The farm house itself was bought at auction by Mr Alan Allen in 1956. Bert Dunkley died a short time later.

Mrs Dunkley and her daughter, Christine, pictured outside their newly acquired farm

Bert Dunkley in front of his farm with his horse and cart

Manor Farm House, 2009

Manor Farm, South View

Manor Farm House dates back to at least the 17th century. At the time of inclosure (1819) it belonged to Robert Cave, a substantial farmer and the second largest landholder in the parish after the Duke of Grafton. It was first described as Manor Farm in the Trade Directories in 1910 when it was occupied (but not owned) by Alfred Comber, farmer. In 1918 the farmhouse and approximately 57 acres of land in the north east of the parish were sold to Frederick William Giddings, farmer and confectioner.

Although Mr Giddings appears to have been living at Manor Farm in 1924, it was later let first to Mr F J Webb and then to Mr A T Webb, both farmers. Mr Giddings also owned other property in the village including various cottages and Roade Boot Shop, which was in front of the farmhouse to the left of the present gate (see Businesses and Shops). In 1948, ownership of the property and 86 acres of land passed from F W Giddings to his son Donald Victor Giddings, a 'gentleman farmer' who lived at Manor Farm with his family.

In 1952 Mr D V Giddings sold the farm and other property in Roade to Pianoforte Supplies Ltd. The house was acquired by Mr W C ('Chappie') Gross, a Director of PSL, and the land behind it was turned into the cricket field. The farmland was retained by PSL and later incorporated in Burman Farms Ltd.

Clearing Cherry Orchard behind Manor Farm for the cricket field

Brown's Lodge, Church End

Brown's Lodge appears on the 1720s map of the village and was then a farmhouse belonging to the Grafton Estate. In 1817 the house and just under 64 acres of land were sold to Sir William Wake and the proceeds were used to defray the Duke's inclosure expenses. The name Brown's Lodge may refer to a farmer and gamekeeper called James Brown who is thought to have lived there around 1861. The following 'nonsense rhyme' about him was composed around 1863 by the Revd Maze Gregory, probably aided by his friend Drury Wake:

Brown's Lodge, 1988

> *There was a good keeper named Brown*
> *Who would shoot his best friend for a crown*
> *And then with a grin, would take off his skin*
> *This friendly old keeper called Brown*

Sir Hereward Wake (the 13th Baronet) sold the house and the paddock behind it to his tenant, John H Bailey, in 1923 but retained the rest of the land, which adjoins Courteenhall. Mr Bailey continued to keep cows, renting land from the Wakes. He delivered milk in the village, ladling it into customers' jugs from a churn carried by bicycle. After the death of John's son, Arnold, in 1955, Brown's Lodge was sold to the Whattons, who kept pigs there. Subsequent owners kept horses and ponies but most of the farm buildings have now been converted for residential use.

White House Farm, London Road (before modernisation)

White House Farm, Woodleys Farm and Thorpewood Farm

The Wakes also owned White House Farm, Thorpewood Farm and Woodleys Farm (formerly the New Inn) and have retained the land as part of Courteenhall Farms. The Thorpewood and White House farmhouses were sold and Woodleys Farm is now a day nursery.

The White House was once the stationmaster's house but had to be moved when the loop line to Northampton was laid in the early 1880s. The house was transported to its present site by carrier's cart. It was the first poultry farm in Roade and later a dairy farm.

Woodleys Farm, formerly the New Inn but renamed after the field behind it

Thorpewood Farm

Farms and smallholdings in 1940

In 1940 there were over 15 farms and smallholdings in Roade. The following were listed in the 1940 Kelly's Directory:

Abbott & Son, farmers
[Hartwell Rd, on the site of Three Ways]

Ayers, Percy, poultry farmer, Palm House
[The Leys]

Bailey, Jn. Hy. farmer, Brown's Lodge
[Church End]

Clarke, Percy Stokes, farmer, Wood Leys Farm

Cooper, Albt. King, farmer, The Laurels
[Hartwell Rd]

Cozens, Rt. Jas. farmer, Burman Farm
[Bretts Lane]

Dunkley, Albt. Chas. smallholder, Elm Farm, High St

Dunkley, Benj. farmer, Hyde Farm

Gardner, Fredk. Ralph, farmer, Thorpewood Farm

Molcher, Harry Arth. poultry farmer, 2 Yew Tree Terrace

Moore, Jn. Charlton, poultry farmer, London Rd

Parish & Son, poultry farmers, The Bungalow
[Ashton Rd]

Scotts, Wltr. Hoyland, farmer, White House Farm

Smith, Chas. Hy. smallholder, Highlands, Ashton Rd

Webb, Alfd. Thos. farmer, Manor Farm
[tenant of F W Giddings]

Ray Parish outside Vine Cottage in White Hart Yard, 1932

Ray Parish (left) and Frank Dunkley 1932

H Parish's stall with customers queuing for eggs during World War II

Also in Roade at that time, though not mentioned in the Directory, was Orchard Farm (between White Hart Yard and Butlin's Lane), then run by Ray Parish's father, Sid. As well as fruit trees, Sid had cows, horses, pigs and poultry. He was also a butcher, coal merchant, haulier and horse dealer. Sid's brother, Arthur, lived nearby and was the village carrier.

Horace Parish, brother of Sid and Arthur, had a poultry farm on Ashton Road and a stall in the Fish Market in Northampton. Later he supported his nephew Ray's greengrocer's shop and stall.

Farms in 2009

Hyde Farm is now the only substantial farm based in Roade, as much of the farmland belongs to Courteenhall Farms and Burman Farms Ltd.

Allotments

It is possible to trace the origins of allotments back over two hundred years - they derive from the inclosure legislation of the 18th and 19th centuries. The word 'allotment' originates from land being allotted to an individual under an inclosure award. Allotments, as we know them, were often provided for the benefit of the landless poor who had suffered as a result of inclosure. Around 1830 the land along Blisworth Road which belonged to the two village charities was let to the poor in allotments of a quarter to half an acre, according to the size of the tenants' families. By the 1890s Sir Herewald Wake (the 12th Baronet) was letting allotments along Northampton Road *'at one half the rent formerly paid for indifferent allotments'*, having 'cut up the best fields' of one of his farms to do so.

The allotments are the dark patch at the top left of this 1970s aerial view

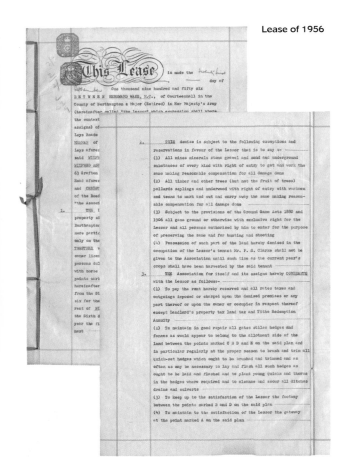

Lease of 1956

The only allotments in Roade now are on land leased from Courteenhall Estate and situated off Northampton Road, opposite the old cricket field. The allotments provided by the Wakes once covered a larger area including the site of the houses on the east side of Northampton Road but demand for them gradually decreased. On 21st September 1956 'Hereward Wake, M.C., of Courteenhall' (later the 14th Baronet) leased 2.8 acres to ten named members of the Roade Allotment Holders Association. The rent was £9 per year. By 1977 the area had been reduced to 1.5 acres. It is now slightly smaller still but demand is increasing again and there is now a waiting list.

The wording of the lease regarding the rights and obligations of the two parties makes interesting reading. Apart from owning *all mines minerals stone gravel sand and underground substances of every kind* the landlord maintained hunting rights over the land. The Association was required *to brush and trim all quick-set hedges*, *'lay and flash'* the hedges and *'cleanse and scour all ditches.'* The current Allotment holders pay rent calculated *'per ten pole plot'*.

Allotments are a diminishing asset in this country and Roade is fortunate to have this facility.

Pete Holden at work on his allotment, 2009

CHAPTER 19

Conclusion

In conclusion, we end with a selection of images which will stir a few memories within the village and beyond.

At play on The Green, 1950s

On yer bikes! Keith Dunkley and Brenda Sturgess (Barby)

The village Bobby: PC Theo (Jack) Neesham, 1952-56

Village lads on their bikes, 1952

Left to right: Clarence Puttnam, Paddy Howard, Bernard Webster, Richard Johnson, Donald Abbott, John Neesham and Denis Connolly

No health and safety then! Roade and Courteenhall Guides at Castle Ashby camp, early 1950s

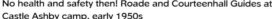

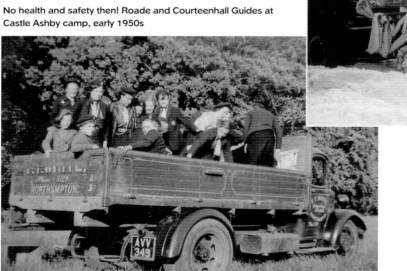

Snowbound, 1963

Oh, Happy Days! 1980

At the Church Fete held in the garden of Manor Farm House: 1.Christopher Cowap 2.Duncan Webster 3.Nicholas Cowap 4.Adrian Webster 5.Jackie Hall 6.Lisa Dredge 7.Tracey Dredge 8.Sindie Johnson 9.Emma Nichamin 10.Trevor Phillips 11.Adele Gearey 12.Tracey Lowe 14.Rachel Antoine

'Did I tell you …?' Madge Wickens (left) and Maisie Curtis

Outdoor girls

Left to right - Back row: Edith Pell, Millie Henman, Nora Gray, Iris Lamb, Margaret Cooper

Front row: Mary Smith, Irene Gray, Jane Clarke

Another happy day! 1937 Coronation of George VI

Left to right: Frank Dunkley, Harry Clarke, Denis Hillyard, Stan Tapp, Ernie Walker, Tom Oakey, Jim Whitlock, Walter Denny, Bob Cozens and Ken Oakey

Ladies night out

Left to right: Mabel Barford (from Wootton), Ruth Haycock (from Hartwell), Mary Smith, Jean Gray, Nora Gray, Cath Walker, Gwen Luck and Mrs Johnson

Dedicated followers of fashion! St. Mary's Junior Church Outing to London 19th October 1974

Left to right: Brenda Barby, Janice Andrew, Joanne Phillips, Lesley Phillips, Paula Phillips, Pat Moore, Stephanie Tipler, Kay Middleton and Penny Hall

Skegness outing, 1920

This photo includes Job Sturgess (front row, extreme left), Harry Nichols (middle right wearing boater) and Dick Alsop (rear extreme right) probably on a church outing

Mates on the beach, 1939
Left to right: Frank Clarke, Tom Smith and unknown

Red Cross Group, 1956
Left to right: Isabel Watford, Maureen Collins, Cynthia Botwood, Doris Baxter, Margery Botwood, Frances Roberts, Mrs Coward, Mrs Oakey, Mrs Webb, Iris Anderson, Kathleen Grose, Renee Malin

WI group, c.1970

Group outing, probably PSL, early 1950s

Lady Hesketh opening the Darby and Joan Club, 1952

Humphrey Family, 1954

Left to right - Back row:
Ethel Humphrey,
Jesse Higgins,
Bill Humphrey,
Derek Humphrey,
Mary Humphrey

Front row: May Kightley,
Elizabeth Higgins,
Sarah Higgins

Shipman Family

Left to right - Back row: Phyllis, Ted, Betty

Front row: Rita, George, Mrs Shipman, Emily and Kathleen

Choral Society in 1938

The photograph includes the Primary School Headmaster Mr Maxwell, (centre), Bill Malin, Bert Coward, Mr Jelley, Harry Curtis, Dick Alsop, Harry Nichols, Eva Gray, Mrs Webb, Mrs Tarry, Mrs Tew, Mrs Coward

Community Choir, keeping up the tradition

Ellen Lane with her granddaughter,
Margaret Lane (Patrick)

Mrs Eva Gray (left) and Mrs Abbott

Claude Grahame-White landed in Roade during the first London to Manchester Air Race, 1910

MR. CLAUDE GRAHAME WHITE
Ready for Flight.

[Series No. 3838

Mary Able (centre) 'putting on the style', c.1900

Above: Highfield House, 18 Hartwell Rd, under construction in 1930. Built for Mr Alsop of Dennis, Faulkner & Alsop, Solicitors in Northampton. The builders are, from the left, Stan Robinson, 'Sixer' Clarke and Jack Skears. It was purchased by the Church as the new Vicarage in 1953.

Left: At the pump, The Leys, 1930

Group outside the Cock Inn

Left to right: Charlie Chaplin, Bernard Blackmar, Horace Smith, Don Gray, Cecil Denny, Roger Oakey, Fred Chaplin, Harry Smith, Jim Howard, Sam Dunkley, Stan Rogers

School group at the War Memorial at the unveiling of the names of the Second World War casualties, 6th June 1948

Left to right: Roger Goode, Margaret Lane, Carole Mann, Alan King, Keith Thomas, John Summers, Mary Sturgess, Beulah Wilson, Pauline Smart

ROADE'S FUTURE

From the A508, even the most perceptive passer-by would be unlikely to notice anything out of the ordinary about Roade. It seems just one more respectable ribbon development straddling a road and rail crossing-point. But Roade has a real, living identity, as any diversion down the High Street or along Hyde Road would soon show. It is considered by planners to be a 'vibrant community,' 'one of the most sustainable Local Service Centres in the District'.

Any villager hearing such accolades may well fear for the future. Though organic change is inevitable and welcome, over-development imposed from outside can easily destroy a community. It is hoped that the images in this book convey some of the depth, the individuality, the quirkiness, unpretentious beauty and variety that the village held and still holds, and highlight the need to preserve it. Roade is the creation of thousands of individuals, themselves mostly forgotten, whose work lives on to benefit current and future residents. Long may it retain its distinctive character!

View of Roade from the west

Roade is the creation of thousands of individuals, themselves mostly forgotten, whose work lives on to benefit current and future residents.

Long may it retain its distinctive character!

Index of Names

Names in brackets after surname indicates name change after the date of the photograph.

Names in brackets preceded by 'née' indicates maiden name.

Photographs are in bold type. Figures in brackets ( ) indicate the number of photographs on that page in which the person is included.

Acknowledgements

Since its formation in 2005, Roade Local History Society has been collecting photographs and documents for a village historical archive. These have all been scanned and stored on computer for safekeeping and future reference. The photographs featured in this book were selected from our still growing database of nearly 2,000 images, many over a century old. Some were scratched or badly faded and these have been restored for greater clarity.

We have spent many months selecting photos and researching background and facts to create the text. It has been our objective to give a balanced view of the village, its people and its history. We particularly wanted to produce a book that could be 'dipped into' as time allowed and attract readers both young and old.

Though great efforts have been made to achieve accuracy and trace ownership, it is almost inevitable that errors will remain - for which we apologise in advance. We would be very glad to receive corrections or amendments from readers. Further material for the archive would also be most welcome, especially as we hope to produce additional publications in the future.

We are extremely grateful for the generous grant from the Local Heritage Initiative, now administered by the Heritage Lottery Fund, which has enabled us to purchase recording, computer, printing and display equipment, and to design and print this book.

Special thanks go to Clare Griffiths of Elpeeko Ltd., our printer, for her professional help with book design and layout, and to Fred To who helped with the refurbishment of some of the old photos. We also thank staff at Northamptonshire Record Office, Northampton Central Library Local Studies Department and Northampton Chronicle & Echo who have all been very helpful and provided more photographs and documents. Thanks also to English Heritage for permission to use 'Aerofilm' aerial photos of the village, to 78 Derngate Northampton Trust who permitted use of photographs from their 'Janet Bassett-Lowke' collection, to Michael Heaton and Sue Blake, respective archivists of Spratton Local History Society and Grafton Regis Millennium Project, and to Nigel Elliott for computer assistance.

Finally this book would not have been possible without the generous help and donations from the many Roade residents who have helped in countless ways by recalling details and incidents and providing photographs and memorabilia of village people and scenes. Our thanks go to them all.

Bill Hudson

Alastair Inglis

Sheila Fitchett

Carol Denton

Vivian and Stephen Blyth